THE
CUSTOMER
RULES

LEE COCKERELL spent his career in the hospitality business, working at Hilton & Marriott before joining Disney. He was responsible for the operations of the Walt Disney World Resort in Orlando for ten years, and now consults with organizations around the world on customer service. Lee's first book *Creating Magic* focused on leadership excellence.

THE CUSTOMER RULES

The 39 Essential Rules

for Delivering

Sensational Service

LEE COCKERELL

P

PROFILE BOOKS

First published in Great Britain in 2013 by
PROFILE BOOKS LTD
3A Exmouth House
Pine Street
London EC1R 0JH
www.profilebooks.com

First published in the United States of America in 2013 by
Crown Business, an imprint of Random House Inc., New York

1 3 5 7 9 10 8 6 4 2

Printed and bound in Great Britain by
Clays, Bungay, Suffolk

A CIP catalogue record for this book is available from the
British Library.

ISBN 978 1 78125 122 5
eISBN 978 1 84765 978 1

The paper this book is printed on is certified by the © 1996 Forest
Stewardship Council A.C. (FSC). It is ancient-forest friendly. The
printer holds FSC chain of custody SGS-COC-2061

For
Priscilla

CONTENTS

INTRODUCTION
Be Nice!

At a recent family gathering in my home, the grown-ups were trading stories about companies that provide good customer service and those that don't. Out of curiosity, I asked my then twelve-year-old granddaughter, Margot, what she thought were the most important rules for great service. Without a moment's hesitation, she said, "Papi, the first rule is 'Be nice!'"

Out of the mouths of babes! I've spent my whole adult life thinking about service, beginning with teenage stints working in a drugstore and a lumberyard in a small Oklahoma town and culminating in my last corporate position as executive vice president of operations at Walt Disney World, where I oversaw a workforce of forty thousand people, resort hotels with more than thirty thousand rooms, four theme parks, two water parks, five golf courses, a shopping village, a nighttime entertainment complex, a sports and recreation complex, and more operations. Along the way, I held positions that included army cook, banquet waiter, food and beverage control clerk, director of food and beverages for Hilton Hotels (including the Waldorf-Astoria), director of restaurants at a Marriott, general manager of another Marriott, and senior executive at Disney in Paris and Orlando.

Throughout these forty-plus years in the hospitality industry, I never stopped searching for better ways to serve customers. Yet despite all the vital lessons I learned over those years from hard experience, brilliant colleagues, and mentors alike, I never heard the basic truth about service expressed as succinctly or as accurately as in Margot's two words.

"Be nice" packs a wallop. Look up "nice" in a dictionary and you find terms like *friendly, polite, pleasant, appealing, kind, considerate, well mannered, refined,* and *skillful.* Who wouldn't want to be surrounded by such qualities when doing business? Margot's first word, "be," is also profound. As I thought about her wise answer, I realized that great service is not just about what we do; it's also about what we *are.* You can have the best policies, procedures, and training in the world, but if the people you entrust to carry them out don't have what it takes—forget it. Don't get me wrong, what you *do* is also vital, and many of the Customer Rules in this book are about exactly that—what to do and how to do it. But *being* comes before doing, and the quality of a person's being—his or her attitude, personality, demeanor, and other factors—is crucial in delivering superior service. As retail consultant Liz Tahir puts it, "There is no way that the quality of customer service can exceed the quality of the people who provide it." Both aspects of great service, being and doing, are addressed in this book.

Think of it this way: Let's say you're a customer, and the staff person you're doing business with does everything by the book and completes the transaction efficiently and satisfactorily, but he is unfriendly, indifferent, condescending, and obviously counting the seconds until the workday ends. Now imagine doing business with someone who makes a mistake but graciously apologizes, corrects the problem, and treats you with courtesy and respect because she's happy to be where she is, serving you. Which company will you return to?

The Customer Rules is both a perfect companion to my first book, *Creating Magic: 10 Common Sense Leadership Strategies from a Life at Disney*, and a logical follow-up. Whereas *Creating Magic* was geared to leaders and aspiring leaders, *The Customer Rules* is relevant to everyone from the highest echelons of management to the frontline troops who interact directly with customers or clientele. It's applicable not just to customer service reps, but to salespeople and servers, tech support analysts and repair workers, desk clerks and ticket takers, delivery personnel and janitors, and even investment bankers, lawyers, teachers, doctors, nurses, and other professionals. *Creating Magic* made the important point that anyone at any level can exercise leadership. But leaders can lead only when there is at least one person who follows. By contrast, anyone and everyone in a company can—and should—be responsible for serving the organization's customers, whether they do so face-to-face, over the phone, or from the distance of a manager's office or an executive suite.

The Customer Rules is focused entirely on one ultimate goal: to help you, no matter what your position or job title, serve customers with such consistency, integrity, creativity, and sincerity that they will not only keep coming back for more, but eagerly recommend your business to their friends, families, and colleagues. It draws upon everything I've learned, from my days as a frontline service provider to my years as a top-tier executive at companies with worldwide reputations for service, and from my experience as a consumer with a lifelong habit of observing how some businesses provide excellent service and others fail at that basic task. The end result is thirty-nine easy-to-follow yet essential Rules that can improve service at every level of a company's operation. If you interact directly with customers, you'll learn how to deliver the kind of superior service that makes you an indispensable asset to the company that employs you. If you're a manager or executive, you'll learn how to create service-driven policies and procedures and hire, orient, and train employees who will win your team or company the most valuable revenue-boosting asset you could wish for: a reputation for superior service.

The principles revealed in this book apply to any

industry and any company, large or small, private or public, profit or not-for-profit. They have proved just as effective in multinational corporations like Disney and Marriott as in local shops and online retailers. They work whether the product is as high-tech as a tablet computer, as complex as health care, or as basic as shoes or coffee. The Rules are presented in concise, bite-size chapters so you can read one or more in minutes, absorb the basic lessons, and put them into practice immediately.

At the end of the day, everything a business leader does is in the service of customer service. That has always been the case, and based on current trends, customer service will be even more crucial to companies' success in the coming years. In today's highly competitive marketplace, a business needs more than excellent products, good technical service, efficient procedures, and more competitive prices to win customers. It also needs to truly connect with its customers through authentic, human-to-human interactions that satisfy not only their practical needs, but their emotional wants. "The advent of global competition, customers' access to reliable information and their ability to communicate with each other through social media has meant that the customer is now in command," writes Stephen Denning, author of *The Leader's Guide to Radical Management*. "The shift goes beyond the firm paying more attention to customer service: it means orienting everyone and everything in the firm on providing more value to customers sooner."

Denning is right when he calls the present period "the Age of Customer Capitalism." Today, the power has shifted from the seller to the buyer. That's why I chose a title with a double entendre. The customer always rules, and there are Rules for winning customers, keeping customers, and turning loyal customers into advocates and emissaries for your business. This isn't just some feel-good business platitude. Your customers are your single source of revenue and profit; without them your company would go out of business and you'd be out of a job. If you follow the Rules in *The Customer Rules*, you will better serve your customers and your bottom line. Even my twelve-year-old granddaughter could tell you that.

THE
CUSTOMER
RULES

Rule #1

Customer Service Is Not a Department

If there's one thing I've learned in my forty-plus years in the business world, it's that customer service is far more than a department name or a desk that shoppers or clients go to with problems and complaints. It's not a website, or a phone number, or an option on a pre-recorded phone menu. Nor is it a task or a chore. It's a *personal responsibility.* And it's not the responsibility only of people called customer service reps. It's the responsibility of everyone in the organization, from the CEO to the newest and lowest-ranking frontline employee. In fact, *everyone* in the company should be thought of as a customer service rep, because in one way or another each of them has some impact on, and bears some responsibility for, the quality of the customer experience. Even if you never see or speak to a customer (or potential customer), you need to treat everyone with whom you interact—your vendors, your creditors, your suppliers, and so on—with sincerity and respect. Trust me, the great service you give them will ultimately trickle down to your customers.

Great service serves bottom-line business objectives. Sounds simple, but I constantly meet executives who don't understand that. They say things like "I'm in the commodity business, and it's all about the product." I tell them that they'd *better* have a great product, because the most extraordinary customer service in the world won't compensate for a bad one. But then I tell them that unless their product is the only one of its kind on the planet (and will *always* be the only one), good quality alone won't guarantee long-term profits. Time and again, customer service has been shown to be the best way to distinguish an outstanding company or organization from its competitors. Let's face it, no matter what business or industry you're in, there's probably someone—or *many* someones—who offers more or less the same product or service you do. But if you provide the same product *plus* personal service that feels authentic, you will have a leg up. No matter what business you're in, great service is a competitive advantage that costs you little or nothing but adds huge value for your customer. And it's one advantage you can't afford to pass up, because in today's highly competitive marketplace your customers will leave you in a heartbeat if your service doesn't measure up. Don't take my word for it; look at the research. In one study, customers were asked why they stopped doing business with a company. Forty-three percent named "negative experience with a staff person" as the main reason for taking their business elsewhere, and 30 percent said they moved on because they were made to feel they were not a valued customer.

My point is that most people *expect* quality products and services. It's the lowest common denominator. But if your company gives people the products or services they want *and* customer service that exceeds their expectations, you have an unbeatable combination, and one your competition can't easily imitate. Don't get confused about the difference between the services you sell and *customer service*. Services are what consumers come to you for and pay for. Customer service encompasses the entire experience, from the moment a person logs on to your website or walks through your front door until the moment they log off or walk out. It's what brings the human factor into a transaction. Some hardened number types scoff at the notion of the human factor. But as I've learned over the course of decades working at some of the most profitable companies in the world, the emotional element is as important as—even *more* important than—the money that changes hands. That is why it should be delivered not just competently, but with ultimate respect, sincerity, and care.

Some managers and executives turn up their noses at the whole idea of service. They believe it's too "soft" for someone in their position of importance to think about, what with all the decisions they have to make and bottom lines they have to meet and the competitors breathing down their necks. Creating better products, building fresh ad campaigns, pioneering new technologies or markets—those tasks feel sexy to them. They get their juices flowing. To them, customer service *is* a department. It's something they can delegate to nice people who get along well with others. They couldn't be more misguided.

That is why *everyone* in a company should be considered part of the customer service department. Several years ago, when I was in charge of operations at Disney World, we changed the title of our frontline managers to "guest service manager" and required them to get out of the office and spend 80 percent of their shift in the operations, providing service support to their direct reports. Overnight, our guest satisfaction scores rose sharply. So whether you're the CEO, a midlevel manager, or the head of a small department, give your team members—and yourself!—responsibilities and titles that reflect their role in pleasing the customer.

Great service does not cost any more money than average or poor service. Yet the returns it delivers are spectacular. So invest in your company's commitment to service by making it part of every employee's job description and the guiding light of your entire operation.

You Win Customers One at a Time and Lose Them a Thousand at a Time

There's an old saying in business: "You win customers one at a time, and you lose them one at a time." It's outdated. In the age of social media, you can easily lose customers a thousand—even a million—at a time. With a few keystrokes, one unhappy, frustrated, ticked-off customer can now tell her whole e-mail list, all her Facebook friends, and everyone who reads her blog or follows her on Twitter why they should not do business with you. She can voice her outrage into a smartphone and put it up on YouTube with clever graphics. With a little creativity, she can even go Michael Moore on you and shoot a mini-documentary, complete with music and special effects, and generate enough viral buzz to do serious damage to your business. One major airline found this out the hard way when they made soldiers returning from Afghanistan pay baggage fees for their fourth bag. The soldiers made a video of the incident and put it up on YouTube. Within a day, the airline received thousands of complaints and was forced to back down.

True, satisfied customers can also spread the word about what they *like* about a company. But will they? Maybe, if they're truly blown away by how great you are. But angry people are far more motivated to shout about their feelings, and furious exposés get a lot more attention than glowing testimonials. Humans are wired to pay more attention to the negative than the positive— it's an evolutionary mechanism designed to keep us safe from danger. It's why drivers slow down to look at car wrecks, not at Good Samaritans helping someone fix a flat tire. It's why we remember warnings a lot better than we do recommendations. It's built into our DNA.

I know about that dynamic from my own experience. I see good service all the time, but I don't always go out of my way to write about it. However, when that same major airline once greeted a reasonable request of mine with a shocking and immediate "No," I quickly posted a detailed description of my experience on my website blog.

Here's what happened. I had decided to combine some speaking engagements with a vacation for my wife and me, plus my son, his wife, and their three kids. The arrangement involved flying from Orlando to Boston, then on to Paris, and later from Paris to Johannesburg, South Africa, before returning to Orlando. I booked the flights through the airline, and let me tell you it was not cheap. About a month before the trip, I received an attractive invitation to give a speech in Boston. All it required was a slight change in my travel schedule. Not wanting to give up the opportunity or the fee, I told the rep that I wanted to cancel the Orlando to Boston segment of my itinerary and then board the Boston to Paris flight with my current ticket. That's all. I didn't ask for any money back for the unused flight. I didn't want to rearrange any of the other six tickets. I just wanted *not* to get on one of the flights. I was even willing to pay more, because fares had gone up since I'd bought the tickets. Their answer: "No." I spoke to several customer reps, and all I got was a chorus of "No." Why? Because it's their policy. You can't change *anything*. If you're not on the Orlando to Boston flight, we will cancel the rest of your ticket, they told me. In other words, I had a choice: Either turn down the speaking opportunity or cancel my entire vacation. It is hard to imagine a dumber policy or a more self-defeating response to a request. I now fly with that airline only when there is no other way to get to my destination, even though I've accumulated so many frequent-flier miles with them that I'm often upgraded. But the upgrade is just one of their services, like online check-in. They don't seem to understand the difference between services like those and respectful, competent customer service with a human touch.

In my own small way, I am sending a message to

that airline that shoddy service exacts a high cost. I tell that story in my speeches and workshops, often contrasting it with happy stories of flying other airlines that consistently do a great job of customer service.

The point is, every time a customer comes into contact with your business, whether in person, on the phone, or on your website, it's a moment of truth. Your reputation is about to get either better or worse. If you do something to tick off your customer at that moment of truth, you can bet hers won't be the only business you lose. Do something that adds value at that moment of truth, and he will look forward to coming back and will tell others about you. Do something that adds a *lot* of value, and that customer might be so stunned by your sincere, thoughtful, friendly, resourceful service that she'll go straight to her computer and tell the world. Satisfied customers are the best marketing staff you can possibly have. They, not your advertisements, are your true messengers. If that airline's service was half as good as its commercials, I would still be a happy customer.

Rule #3

Great Service Follows the Law of Gravity

It's a simple law of nature: The service ethos starts at the top. From there, it works its way down to every level of an organization. This is not a mere trickle-down effect; it flows quickly and surely, more like a waterfall than a faucet.

Whenever you see truly great service, whether it's from a local coffee shop or a global fast-food chain, a small financial services firm or a multinational bank, a rural clinic or a gigantic city hospital, it's a good bet that a senior person has made customer service an integral part of his or her strategy. Unless the people at the top of an organization, division, or department are dedicated to developing and maintaining superior service, it won't happen. They have to create the right agenda, allocate the necessary resources, establish the appropriate priorities, and set the proper tone. The best of those leaders also serve as role models, demonstrating the attributes of great service with every word, action, and communication—not just with customers, but with suppliers, colleagues, employees, and everyone else who has an impact on the way business is done.

In my experience, the leaders of companies that *don't* provide good service—the companies that consumers complain about the most—usually have the least people-oriented strategy. Their focus is on products, sales, marketing, and other business concerns. Those are all vital, of course, but in today's world they're not enough to drive long-term success. Managers have to recognize that sustained profits depend on their ability to generate consistent, ongoing, excellent service that keeps customers coming back and singing their praises.

During my career, I worked for three companies where sensational service generated spectacular business results: Hilton, Marriott, and Disney. In all those places, the service ethos flowed from the top. At Walt Disney World, for instance, when Judson Green, the head of parks and resorts, decided to radically change the corporate culture, he stood up in front of seven thousand managers in Orlando and told them exactly what he wanted to see happen. Then he went to Disneyland in California and on to France and Japan, laying out the same vision for the employees in each of those facilities. As someone who played a major role in designing and executing the plan, I can tell you that Judson's 100 percent commitment was contagious—as was mine and that of every other leader, at every level and at every stage of the rollout. Slowly but surely, everyone in the company learned that just having outstanding parks and the most recognized name in recreation and entertainment was not enough. Customers also need the emotional satisfaction of being treated like the most important people in the world. That add-on essentially became the Disney World brand.

No matter what your role or title, you can do a lot more to spread the ethos of service in your department, or within your own team, than you might think you can. Yes, the law of service gravity begins at the top, but the top is wherever you are. If you go to work every morning focused on customer service, you'll be surprised how powerful your example is and how quickly your mind-set will flow to those both under and around you. Remember, role modeling is by far the best teacher, and you are being watched every second of the day.

A few years ago, I read a book titled *Leading Out Loud*. It had a big impact on me. Its basic premise is that great leaders speak loudly and often about what they want their organizations to focus on and what employees are expected to do to achieve those goals. It's not unlike parenting. All parents know that they have to speak up over and over again to make sure their children understand and adopt the right values, behaviors, and social skills.

Whether it's raising children to grow up with integrity and respect for themselves and others or inspiring employees and colleagues to serve customers with excellence, you have to lead out loud. It will be a win-win for everyone concerned: you, your team, your customers, and everyone with a stake in your bottom line.

Rule #4

Don't Get Bored with the Basics

I once used this rule as the subject of a blog post. I wrote about how one day you will wake up and realize that the small things in your life—like building warm, trusting relationships—were really the big things. I received more comments on that post than on anything else I have ever put up on the Web. The great majority thanked me for reminding them of how important the basics are and how easy it is to forget them.

Great companies and successful individuals alike keep a keen eye on the basics at all times. Like great athletes, they know that mastering the fundamentals makes all the difference between success and failure—that you can't expect to hit a game-winning home run before you've mastered swinging the bat. In business, the seemingly small things are easy to overlook, but they can set your company apart from the competition and in turn increase your sales, your repeat business, and your bottom line. Why? *Because to customers, the small things are the big things.*

Take common hospitality, for example. Conrad Hilton once said, "It has been, and continues to be, our responsibility to fill the earth with the light and warmth of hospitality." Can you get more basic than that? The Greek word for "hospitality" is *philoxenia*, which literally means "love of strangers." Hospitable people love to offer the comforts of home to family, to friends, and especially to strangers. They have a gift for sensitivity and courtesy; they know how to make people feel at ease and welcome. The ancient Greeks believed that providing hospitality to strangers pleased the gods. I don't know about the gods, but I assure you it will please the customers who come to your business.

If you want to know how important the basics are, watch a good hospital staff in action. When my wife, Priscilla, was in the Orlando Regional Medical Center (Orlando Health) for sixty-four days in 2008 and 2009, I sat with her in her room day and night. One day, I noticed that every nurse carefully used the disinfectant hand wash as he or she entered and exited the room. Sounds obvious, right? What could be more basic, particularly in a hospital, than washing our hands, something our mothers nagged us to do when we were growing up? But this is a huge deal because, as you can imagine, the simple act of hand washing dramatically reduces infection rates, which helps patients return to good health more quickly and sometimes even saves lives. It seems like a small thing, but the payoff is big: not only healthy, happy patients, but lower costs to the hospital and insurance companies.

Cleanliness may not be next to godliness, but it is— or at least it should be—a business basic everywhere. Obviously, that's especially true if you're running a hotel, a restaurant, or any other place food is served; when it comes to the food we put in our mouths, it may be the most important basic there is. But cleanliness is a key basic no matter what you're selling—whether it's insurance policies or advertising space or legal services or anything else. After all, which company do you think clients will do repeat business with, the one that makes its pitch in a sparkly clean office or the one whose offices and meeting rooms are a filthy mess? That's why Bill Marriott, for whom I once worked, used to say, "Keep it clean and keep it friendly, and everything will work out just fine." Walt Disney said basically the same thing. It seems almost too simple to bear mentioning. But that's exactly the point.

Hand in hand with cleanliness are its close cousins, personal appearance and hygiene. Again, this is about as basic as it gets. Make sure everyone looks good and smells good. If they don't, make sure you talk to them about it. I know, it's a conversation no one likes to have, but the more you procrastinate, the more customers your unkempt employee will cost you. Your mother didn't have trouble saying, "I hope you don't think you are going out looking like that," did she? Neither should a manager—or a colleague, for that matter. Every company, of course, has its own standards for appearance that fit its location, its image, and the customs of its clientele: a salesperson in a vintage clothing store in Brooklyn is not expected to look like the concierge at the Four Seasons in Beverly Hills. The point is to make sure your appearance—and, if you're the boss or manager, your employees' appearance—is consistent with the image you want to project to your customers.

Another basic every business should pay attention to is clear communication. Your communication skills are seen as a measure of your professionalism, intelligence, preparation, and character—all of which are major factors in how the customer, consciously or not, evaluates the company. First and foremost, you and every single person in your company should be able to communicate clearly with customers, both verbally and in writing. Clarity is the essence of communication; when you're clear, there is no room for misunderstanding.

One of the most important communication basics that many companies forget is that it's not enough just to convey important information; you need to convey it consistently and in a timely fashion. Southwest Airlines does this exceptionally well. It is common to hear a message like this on the sound system in their boarding area: "Your plane is arriving about fifteen minutes late, but we will hustle to get you in the air on time." By constantly keeping passengers informed about departure times, delays, and changes in the schedule, they keep the anxiety level low and send the message that they really care.

Here is another example of clear and consistent communication. Manny, the agent at my local car dealership, is always available as soon as I come in for a repair. He explains every detail before the service is done. He stays in constant contact with me while the car is being worked on, to let me know how it's coming along. When he's running behind, he lets me know as quickly as possible so I can adjust my schedule accordingly. In return, I do my part to send car buyers his way, and I posted a message about the dealership's excellent service on my blog. I'll bet I'm not the only one. Sending a timely text or e-mail update lets your customers know that you care.

Another basic all companies need to focus on is thoughtfulness. Make sure to focus on each customer individually and go the extra mile to ask thoughtful questions—and teach your teams, your employees, and your colleagues to do the same. Once, when I brought my car in for servicing, Manny asked me how my book was coming along. I had not been there for about three months, yet he remembered that I was working on this book and was gracious enough to ask about it. Maybe he has a great memory, or maybe he keeps a file of little things like that about his customers. Either way, I must admit he made me feel special when he asked me that question—and that's how you want *all* your customers to feel.

Finally, don't forget knowledge. If you are going to provide great customer service, you and all your employees must know enough to perform your duties and provide customers with the information they need. Do you educate your employees thoroughly before turning them loose on customers? Do you test their knowledge? Many companies have found that adding testing procedures to their training programs dramatically improves employee performance, and that, in turn, boosts customer satisfaction.

To recap the basics:

1. Cleanliness
2. Personal appearance/hygiene
3. Clear communication
4. Thoughtfulness
5. Knowledge

What are some other important basics in your business? If you haven't taken the time to identify them, I strongly recommend that you do. Then, if you're a manager, make sure everyone who works for you masters them and applies them every minute of every day.

Ask Yourself, "What Would Mom Do?"

One day I'm going to write a book titled *Manage Like a Mother*. Throughout my career, I have constantly found myself thinking about what my mother would have done if she'd been in the particular situation I was faced with. I've had great mentors in my life, but she was by far the most responsible for what I became and who I am today. She taught me that to be successful I would have to work hard, and she inspired me by working harder than anyone I've ever known. The fact that she instilled such good habits and so much self-confidence in this dirt-poor college dropout from Bartlesville, Oklahoma, that I was able to carve out a career at the highest levels of the hospitality industry is nothing short of incredible.

I can't possibly know what kind of manager my mother would have been in the corporate world, but I do know that the thought that guided her while she was raising my brother and me—always do the right thing—is one that business leaders would do well to follow. As I climbed the leadership ranks, I found myself trying to live up to that simple standard, with one additional twist. I told myself: Don't do anything you would not want Mom to know about. I strongly recommend that you and everyone involved in serving your customers do the same.

Another lesson from Mom is to make every customer feel comfortable and welcome. Think back to when your own mother taught you to welcome graciously every visitor to your home and every new kid on the block. Moms want their kids to be standout performers but also team players. Customer service is a team sport, so make sure your fellow employees feel included, just as Mom encouraged you to do for the other kids on the playground. Give them inside tips to improve their skills. Encourage them, help them correct their mistakes, and show them appreciation when they do things well. If they behave unprofessionally, show them the better way. If they don't know procedures or how to operate a piece of equipment, teach them. A little "mothering" goes a long way.

You may not have appreciated it at the time, but the lessons your mom taught you while you were growing up are actually terrific business lessons. Look at this list of things mothers typically say, and see if you don't find them to be excellent customer service tips:

* Never ask for something without saying "please" or receive something from another person without saying "thank you."
* Greet people with eye contact and a friendly smile.
* Always say "I'm sorry" when you upset someone or make a mistake.
* Always keep your promises.
* Never tell a lie.
* Don't even think about going out looking like that.
* If you can't say something nice, don't say anything.
* Try to see it from his or her point of view.
* Treat others as you would want to be treated.
* Do it right or don't do it at all.

Employees who act in the spirit of these maxims will invariably provide better customer service—not to mention get along better in life in general.

No matter where you are positioned in the company hierarchy, your career depends to a large extent on showing up to work every morning just as your mother would have liked you to leave the house for school: filled with energy and confidence, exuding a can-do spirit, and sporting a bounce in your step. She'd want you to walk through that door with a drive for excellence and a willingness to persevere in the face of setbacks and disappointments. She'd want you to display not only the skills to play the game exceptionally well, but the ethical foundation to play fair and by the rules (while being impeccably dressed and well-groomed, of course). All moms want their kids to be above average, and in a tough economy you can't afford to be an average performer, so strive to give your customers the kind of service your mom would have bragged about to the neighbors.

Good managers who want to get the most out of their employees can benefit from another trait all good mothers have: long-term vision. Mothers are always thinking about what kinds of adults they want their children to grow up to be. That's why they put so much emphasis on education. That's why they try to instill self-esteem and confidence. That's why they make their kids feel secure and valued from the day they're born. A mom who wants her kids to believe in themselves lets them know in a thousand ways that she believes in them. As a manager, you should be doing the same. Think through what kinds of people you want your employees to be, and educate them accordingly. Build their self-esteem and confidence. Make them feel secure and valued. Show them you believe in them. Doing those things does not guarantee that every employee will turn out to be an excellent performer, of course. Mothers don't have guarantees about their kids, either. But the good ones know how to tip the odds in their favor.

One final suggestion. The next time a customer thanks you for your help, or your boss pats you on the back for a job well done, or you accomplish something you're proud of at work, call up your mother. (If your mother has passed away, imagine speaking to her as if she were still with us.) When she answers, say, "Hi, Mom, something good happened today, and I just wanted to say thank you for everything you did for me and everything you taught me. I now realize that I am where I am because of you." Abe Lincoln couldn't have summed it up better when he said: "All that I am or ever hope to be, I owe to my angel mother."

Rule #6

Be an Ecologist

If you have ever taken the time to read about or study ecology, you understand that ecosystems are carefully balanced and that everything within an ecosystem is important and interconnected. If you leave an environment alone, over time—often a very long time—it will eventually self-regulate. But if you add or take something away, everything else in that environment will ultimately be affected.

Your organization is like an ecosystem, and everything in it is interconnected, just as in the natural environment. In other words, what happens in one area affects every other area to one degree or another. Therefore, everything you do affects the quality of your service. If you want your customers to experience excellent service, pay close attention to every decision you make, every policy you announce, every procedure you introduce, every person you hire, every promotion you award, every e-mail you send, every conversation you have, every hand you shake, and every back you slap. Even something that seems a universe removed from a customer interaction or a point of sale can actually have tremendous repercussions on the service your customers receive, and therefore your bottom line.

When I give speeches and workshops, I often tell audiences that in my years as a manager, my job was to create an ecosystem of service excellence. Then I tell them that in that endeavor my success hinged largely on three things. One was hiring great people; the second was making sure those employees had the expertise, training, and resources to excel at what they did; and the third was leaving them alone to do their jobs without looking over their shoulders or micromanaging them. When I did that, I found that eventually the system would self-regulate, just like a natural ecosystem.

In companies with cultures of great service, the people at the top let their direct reports do their jobs. That frees the bosses to do theirs. For example, when I was running operations at Walt Disney World, I had two great executives named Bud Dare and Jeff Vahle who took care of all the capital projects. With their four-thousand-strong maintenance team, they kept the whole place looking great. Bud was a CPA, and Jeff was an engineer. Since those are two skill sets in which I have zero competence, I left them to do their jobs without interference, and over the years they both excelled, which made me look as good as the parks and resorts. I did the same with Dieter Hannig, who was responsible for all of our food and beverage operations. I had worked in that area myself for twenty-five years, but Dieter knew a whole lot more about getting great meals onto people's tables than I'll ever know, so I ceded that part of the operation to him. Ditto all the other top-notch people I worked with, such as Liz Boice in merchandise and Don Robinson, Erin Wallace, Alice Norsworthy, and Karl Holz in operations. The result was that each one had the freedom to make the kinds of everyday decisions—such as what wine to serve, or how to direct foot traffic, or dozens of other details—that they knew would best enhance the customer experience.

Those executives did their jobs so well that people would ask me, "Lee, with all these great people working for you, what exactly do you do?" The answer was: I was the chief ecologist. I focused on improving the environment and culture at Disney World, but without disrupting the delicate ecosystem. My goal was to nurture a healthy, toxin-free environment where everyone was motivated to do whatever they could to treat each guest like the most important person in the world—and had the skills and means to deliver on that responsibility. I hired and promoted the right people, made sure they were well trained, and created a culture in which everyone knew they mattered and woke up in the morning eager to get to work.

The great thing is that no matter who you are or what position you have in your company, you can be an ecologist. You don't need any special authority or even a single direct report to make your corner of the enterprise a healthy, flourishing environment. Even if the rest of your organization is a mess and suffers from leadership blight, you can still create a Shangri-la among the people around you if you follow the Customer Rules. Don't worry about what everyone else is doing; focus on what you can do to sustain an ecosystem that is centered on satisfying every customer's needs.

Rule #7

Look Sharp

In the early 1970s, when I was a young restaurant manager working at the Philadelphia Marriott, the company founders, J. W. Marriott and his wife, Alice, came into the coffee shop one morning. Mr. Marriott walked right up to me and looked at my badge, which displayed my name and title. "Cockerell, are you the restaurant manager here?"

"Yes, sir," I answered.

He looked me in the eye, grabbed a fistful of my hair, which was hanging over my ears, and said, "Why don't you get a haircut and look like it?"

After I recovered from my near heart attack, I went right down to the hotel barber and got an emergency haircut. The shock and embarrassment made me realize that while long hair may have been in style among my peers at the time, it was *not* the style for successful professionals. From that day on, I paid more attention to my personal appearance. Instead of looking like the guys I once hung out with—guys who were primarily unemployed, playing in bands, and living in their parents' basements—I chose to look like the people with steady jobs and successful careers. I even studied the photos in the company's annual report booklet to see what the top executives looked like, because I wanted to become one of them one day. And I did.

In a perfect world, what you look like, how you dress, or even whether or not you comb your hair would have no bearing on what your customers think of you. But the world is far from perfect, and the fact is that people will make assumptions about you in the first few seconds they spend with you. The average customer is no different, and not only will customers be quick to judge you, they will judge you based on the way they expect a person serving them to look. If your appearance and demeanor are professional, they will assume that the service you provide is professional. If not, they will take their business elsewhere.

If you work in a big company, you've probably been told exactly how you're expected to dress and look. You may not like those standards. You may protest, "That's not me!" Well, maybe it's not you on your off hours, but it *is* you at work—if you want to do your job well and advance to the next level, that is. Think of it as a costume for a role you're playing in a show, and play it to perfection. You can be as quirky and trendy and individualistic as you like when the curtain comes down.

If you're not sure about the personal appearance standards in your workplace—either for yourself or for the people you manage—take a close look at those who are most successful in the field or position you're in. How are they dressed? How do they present themselves? Does their demeanor suggest that they're glad to be there serving customers or wish they were somewhere else? In most cases, you'll find that successful people never look sloppy, unkempt, or disheveled, and you will never see them slump, frown, smirk, or look bored, tired, or sullen. Looking sharp is not just about clothing or grooming. It's also about how you present yourself. So make sure both you and your employees display appropriate body language at all times. Everyone should look alert, attentive, energetic, happy to be there, and eager to serve.

When it comes to service, energy is vital. You may look sharp, but you won't *feel* sharp if you lack physical, emotional, and mental energy. Think about the people you come into contact with on a daily basis. Do you like to do business with those who greet you energetically or the ones who stand there yawning and looking lethargic? Be one of those high-spirited people who wake up raring to go. And if you're in a position of authority, hire people with alertness and vitality—people who look as if they have the energy and drive to go the extra mile for your customers.

If you look sharp, you'll feel sharp, and you'll provide sharp service. At the very least, customers will *perceive* your service as better—and grade your performance higher—simply because you look right for the part. This may not be fair, but it's the way it is.

Rule #8

Always Act Like a Professional

When we hear the word *professional*, we usually think of people who are trained and qualified to undertake specialized tasks and are paid well to perform them. In the past, the term was generally applied only to doctors, lawyers, clergymen, military officers, and high-ranking executives. Today, it's attached to all kinds of occupations and positions, from educators to scientists to real estate agents to athletes. But there is a stark difference between a person who is in a professional position and someone who *acts professionally*. Think of all the professional athletes you have seen acting like spoiled brats. Or professional lawyers who behave like petty thieves. At the same time, think about all the bus drivers, cashiers, and desk clerks who behave like consummate professionals. The point is, professionalism is not about training or job title or pay grade; it is about how you conduct yourself, particularly in the presence of clients, customers, passengers, and patients.

When I speak to audiences on this topic, I always cite the example of waiters and waitresses in Los Angeles restaurants, many of whom are actors or musicians waiting to be discovered. Some of these aspiring performers serve with an air of boredom and resentment, as if they want everyone to know that waiting tables is really beneath them and they're doing it only until they get their big break. Others treat their jobs with respect. They may secretly wish that the meal they're serving will be their last, but they take pains not to show it. Instead, they work hard and treat every customer as if he or she is important. And it pays off. Many well-known entertainers got their first big break by delivering outstanding service to a customer who turned out to be a casting director or a studio executive.

True professionals come to work energized by the passion to excel, no matter what level of responsibility they have at the moment. And they know that if you provide excellence in a world where excellence is rare, the chances of being noticed by the right person skyrocket. This is a secret I learned early in my career, and it's one of the main reasons I got to where I did despite being a college dropout from an Oklahoma farm town. When I had to peel potatoes in the army, for example, I made sure my potatoes had every last piece of skin removed, and I took pride in doing it. I kept that attitude for the rest of my career, and it obviously paid off. Influential people know that the pursuit of excellence is transferable, and if they see you striving for it in one capacity, they know you'll do it in another.

So whether you're currently in your dream job or working somewhere less than ideal so you can pay the bills until a better opportunity knocks, start striving for professional excellence right now.

Professionals care about what they do and the impact they have on each and every customer. They bring a positive, can-do spirit to their work, and customers can tell that they genuinely care about giving the best possible service.

Professionals are inspired, and they are inspiring to others. They are solution-driven, attacking challenges with enthusiasm, pride, and dedication, leaving no *i* undotted and no *t* uncrossed. Professionals are flexible, adaptable, and able to shift gears if life throws them a curveball when they expect a fastball. They are responsible, well prepared, helpful, efficient, trustworthy, highly competent, and always confident. They are ready to do whatever is necessary, regardless of the circumstances or the amount of pressure they're under. When problems persist, so do they, embodying Thomas Edison's attitude about perseverance in the face of setbacks: "I have not failed," the legendary inventor once said. "I've just found ten thousand ways that won't work."

Professionals give their all whether they are tackling a fascinating new challenge or doing something they've done a thousand times; whether they are working behind a closed door or are being watched by the CEO. Think of top-notch athletes: the best of them work as hard in practice as they do with a championship on the line.

Professionals show up—on time and ready to go. If a situation demands that they come in early, or stay late, or give up their usual day off—no problem. They are present and accounted for. In their interactions with coworkers, they are upbeat and positive. They don't indulge in petty gossip; they don't whine when things don't go the way they wish them to; they don't moan about workplace hassles and snafus.

Professionals are self-directed, self-motivated, and self-sufficient, but they also know how to play with others. They partner well and value strong working relationships. They keep their promises, treat their commitments like sacred vows, and are willing to be held accountable.

Although they are highly focused and single-minded in pursuit of results, professionals are not humorless or grim; they take their work seriously, but they don't take *themselves* too seriously. While they are proud of their accomplishments, they are not arrogant or self-important.

Perhaps most important, professionals are always in control. They may not always be able to control the world around them, but they are always in control of themselves, and it shows.

When I started out in my career, I didn't feel like a professional. But as they say in 12-step programs, sometimes you have to fake it till you make it, and that's exactly what I did: I became a good actor. I learned to look like a professional and behave like a professional. I even learned to speak like one, by improving my vocabulary, training myself to use correct grammar, and dropping bad habits like muttering "ummm" and "you know" and "like." Professionals pay attention to what comes out of their mouths.

You've probably heard the saying "Don't dress for the job you have, dress for the one you want." I recommend taking this advice even further: Don't serve as though you have the job you have, serve as though you have the job you want. If you're in a frontline position, act so professionally that customers will think you're the manager; if you're a manager, act so professionally that you'll be mistaken for the owner or the CEO.

Your customers will respect you for it, your boss will respect you for it, and most important, you'll respect yourself for it. And at the end of the day, self-respect is what professionalism is all about.

Hire the Best Cast

Providing great customer service takes more than just flexible policies and adaptable procedures; you also need the right people to *execute* those smart policies and procedures. Otherwise you're like a football coach with a great game plan and lousy players.

Many managers have little or no training in how to interview prospective employees. They typically ask applicants questions that yield little useful information about how the person will actually perform on the job. As a result, they end up making decisions based on little more than a gut feeling. Hiring is too important to be done so haphazardly. That's why *everyone* involved in the employee selection process—not just the folks in human resources—should know how to conduct an interview that will help them select a candidate with a strong commitment to service. No matter what level you occupy in your organization, the better you are at interviewing and selecting employees, the easier your job as a manager will be and the better your customer service will be.

When I first entered management, I was about as good as most managers at hiring new employees. Translation: I didn't really know what I was doing. My first lessons on hiring the right people came from the Gallup organization, which taught me how to determine the talents people had and the ones they *didn't* have. Then I was introduced to Carol Quinn and her Motivation-Based Interviewing method (MBI, see www.hire authority.com). It was a revelation. Quinn had designed the program to be able to distinguish the true A players from applicants who gave impressive interviews but ended up as disappointments on the job. Thanks to her, I changed the way I conducted interviews, and I hired outstanding people for the rest of my career.

One thing I learned is that some of the most frequently asked interview questions are counterproductive; they actually *help* applicants provide the kinds of overly positive responses that make them look better than they really are. For example: "Tell me about a time you went above and beyond to satisfy a customer." Variations on that theme are common, because interviewers think it will reveal something about the prospective hire. The problem is, even the worst employees can come up with at least *one* time they did an exceptionally good job, and there is no way of knowing whether that impressive story they tell you is an example of their typical behavior or the one bright spot in a history of mediocrity. So I stopped asking that kind of question. Instead, I asked about their experience dealing with job challenges or obstacles. For example, I might ask, "Tell me about a specific time you had to deal with an irate customer." Notice the difference. It's a more open-ended invitation. People might respond with the one time they did something exceptional, but they might not. They might remember a time when they did just enough, or they might talk about a customer who was impossible to satisfy or even a time they messed up. They might tell you more than one story. The point is, if you ask questions that can elicit a range of responses, you'll learn a lot more than you will if you ask for their career highlights.

One big mistake people make in staffing is assuming that skill level alone is enough to justify hiring someone. Of course, you need to take the applicant's skills into account, but you should never stop there. You also need to assess two other vital ingredients of great service: attitude and passion.

You've probably heard the saying "Hire the attitude, teach the skill." When I talk about attitude in the context of service, I mean the degree to which people believe they have the power to affect outcomes, even in the face of tough challenges. Stated simply, there are two types of people: those with an "I can" attitude, who believe they can overcome obstacles, and those with a predominant "I can't" attitude, who believe that outcomes are determined mainly by external factors. That second group is likely to shrink in the face of a challenge; convinced that outcomes are out of their control, they see no reason to exert any meaningful effort. As a result, they fail to deliver top-notch performance. By contrast, "I can" individuals relentlessly put forth creative effort in pursuit of solutions, because they believe that success is simply a matter of time and steadfast determination. As Henry Ford, the innovative founder of the Ford Motor Company, once said, "Whether you think you can or you cannot, you're right!" That's why it's crucial to hire people with the right attitude to deal directly with your customers.

But even people with the right skills and an "I can" attitude can come up short when it comes to service if they lack passion. Customers can sense a lack of passion from a mile away, and they'd rather do business with employees who seem motivated and energized than with those who act as if their job is killing them inside. Look for people who will love doing the job you're hiring them to do. Passion for one's work is a powerful motivator. And the best part is, you don't have to light a fire under those who have it, because that fire comes from within. If you want employees who love their work, look for applicants who exude that kind of passion when they first walk in the door and introduce themselves.

When it comes to customer satisfaction, the single most effective strategy is to hire people who have what I call "the triple crown" of customer service—great skill, an "I can do whatever is needed" attitude, and tremendous passion for their work. Taken together, these three add up to the single most indispensable element of great customer service: commitment. This is true for every business or profession under the sun. Committed doctors have more satisfied patients. Committed teachers have more satisfied students. Whether you work in a school or a hospital, a retail chain or an airline, a grocery store or a manufacturing plant, if you want to deliver great service, you need to hire skilled, passionate, can-do people who are committed to giving each and every customer the best possible experience.

Rule #10

Be Your Own Shakespeare

Years ago, I tried to imagine what a perfect trip to Walt Disney World would be like for a typical family of four. I then actually wrote it out in the form of a ten-page story describing a weeklong visit by the fictional Rogers family. Why did I do this? Because I had just moved to Orlando to be senior vice president of resort operations, and the Rogerses' fictional story was essentially a script. I planned to use it to show cast members how to perfectly serve each guest.

Here's how the story went: The family arrives. The valets park their car carefully, the greeters greet them politely, the bell staff take their luggage graciously, and the front desk checks them in efficiently and smoothly. The story went on to describe the perfectly prepared room, followed by pleasant encounters with friendly, well-informed cast members everywhere the Rogerses went: eating at a restaurant, boarding a bus, buying ice cream, riding Space Mountain, and so forth. This five-star performance ended on departure day, with cast members waving good-bye to the beaming Rogers family, who had just had the vacation of their lives.

The act of writing that story gave me a vivid picture of how service excellence would be experienced by guests. I distributed the script to everyone who worked in my area of responsibility so they could turn the vision of perfect service into reality. My cover letter said, among other things, that I hoped the story "will help you visualize and understand what world-class service would look like at Walt Disney World." It became the template for everything I did during my tenure. Whether your job is to answer phone calls or deliver consulting services; whether you're in accounts payable or tech support; whether you're a server in a restaurant or the maître d'; whether you're a bank teller or the bank manager; whether you're a flight attendant or a pilot—you too can create a similar script for what great service should look like.

I often tell people to begin each workday as if they were stepping onstage to perform the show of their lives. I tell them to imagine that the big red curtain is about to go up and there are critics sitting in the front row. I also remind them that a great performance depends on a great script; just ask any producer, director, or actor, and they'll tell you that it all begins with words on a page. So if your goal is a great service performance, you first have to spell out exactly what that would look like. Why not be your own Shakespeare?

Start by imagining the perfect experience for someone coming to your business, no matter what it is, from the moment they arrive in the parking lot, at the front door, in the lobby, or in the reception room to the moment they leave, happy and content and eager to return. What do they see? What do they hear? How do they feel? Think through every detail and what you and your employees—the performers—have to do to make that perfect experience possible. Who does what? When do they do it? What do they say? How do they say it? What are they wearing? What is their attitude? The more detailed you get, the better.

The next step is to share your script with everyone in your team, your department, or even the entire organization. After all, as with a Broadway play or a Hollywood movie, the only way to guarantee a hit production is to make sure the entire cast knows their parts. Of course, if you run a large organization with a cast of thousands, you can't include every tiny detail or your story will end up longer than *War and Peace*. So leave out some details and invite others to fill them in for their own departments. This will encourage people to write their own scripts—a practice that will stimulate creative engagement and ensure that every aspect of the overall performance is covered.

If theater isn't your thing, think of your script as a

recipe. Chefs don't write down their recipes for fun; they do it so that once they have figured out the perfect mix of ingredients, they can reproduce that dish exactly the same way every time. In the same way, once you've perfected your recipe for service, wouldn't you want to make sure you could serve it up consistently, day in and day out?

Of course, while the script or recipe is an indispensable blueprint for consistent performance, it should not be set in stone. Every director and actor (and chef) will tell you that no two performances (or meals) are *exactly* the same, even if no one changes a single line of the dialogue (or a single ingredient). If you have the right cast and have rehearsed them well, you can and should let them improvise once they've mastered the script (see Rule #35, "Be Flexible"). This is particularly important, because your performers will be interacting with unpredictable extras called customers, so they will have to improvise even more than actors on a stage or screen. Plus, circumstances change constantly, so I recommend revising your script from time to time. We did that with my Rogers family story as new services were introduced and new technology became available.

A well-developed script is also a terrific resource for hiring and training. Like a casting director, you can study the script to define what characteristics to look for when you "audition" candidates. For instance, if you are hiring a salesperson, you'll want an extrovert with high energy, a big natural smile, and an ability to interact with a high volume of customers. Your script can help you pick out those qualities because it spells out that "character's" words, appearance, demeanor, and specific actions in more detail than the typical job description.

The bottom line is, do not leave employee performance to chance. Make sure everyone has a script. Like audiences who attend plays and concerts, your customers want excellence every time. A great script ensures that your business will have a long, lucrative run.

Become an Expert at Creating Experts

If you were a patient about to go into surgery, would you rather have an expertly trained, highly experienced surgeon operating on you, or a first-year doctor who barely squeaked through medical school? In the same way, while it may not be a matter of life and death, your customers also want to deal with experts they can trust.

As we learned from my granddaughter, Margot, "Be nice" is the first rule of great service—but it is not the *only* rule. The truth is, customers can be lured and seduced by niceness, but if they don't also receive expertise and competence, they'll take their business elsewhere: someplace where people know what they're doing. In my travels around the world, I have run into an awful lot of nice incompetent managers and nice incompetent employees. I feel sorry for them, because without the training they need to fulfill their roles, these nice folks are missing out on the satisfaction of a job well done.

Once you hire people with the right stuff, you need to teach them your service philosophy and train them to carry out the specific tasks required of them. I often ask my audiences, "How many of your companies have a training and development department?" Almost everyone raises his or her hand. But what few of them realize is that training and development is not a department, it's a responsibility, and one that belongs not just to a few HR reps or training coordinators, but to everyone in the company. I learned that lesson early in my career, when Bill Marriott told me, "The only way to get excellence is with training, education, and enforcement." I've seen those words proven true time and time again; organizations that devote meaningful time and resources to training their employees deliver service better than the rest.

This means educating everyone in the organization about everything the company does, from its mission statement and corporate philosophy to its full line of products and services, even to its business model. Only when employees are solidly grounded in knowledge about the company and its products are they equipped to serve properly when they're face-to-face, voice-to-voice, or keyboard-to-keyboard with your customers. Knowledge is power, and a knowledgeable employee can turn a vaguely interested consumer into a purchasing customer and a onetime customer into a regular customer. We all know how frustrating it is to do business with ill-informed employees. Once, on a business trip, I accidentally backed my rented car into a pole. Because I had a tight schedule and a flight to catch, I phoned the insurance agency's special hotline on the way to the airport to find out how long it would take to do the insurance paperwork when I returned the car. The person who answered the phone had no idea, so he connected me to the help desk. Once the service rep finally picked up, he listened politely, then launched into a rambling list of alternatives—you can do this, or you can do that, or maybe another thing—none of which answered my question. He just kept talking, as if moving his lips might unlock some secret compartment in his brain where the answer was hiding. Finally, I stopped him and repeated what I had said originally: I just need to know how long it will take. He admitted he didn't know. So I asked for the number of the rental return lot. Happily, a friendly woman answered my question without hesitation. "Five minutes maximum," she said. Then she added, "Claims will call you when they have the damage estimate, and you can work out how you want to take care of it. They will take a check, money order, credit card, or cash."

What a relief! She knew exactly what I needed to know, and she gave me the information without beating around the bush. If everyone at that company—especially people at the so-called help desk—had had her expertise, I wouldn't have wasted fifteen minutes before she took care of me in less than sixty seconds. Not only that, the employees I spoke with wouldn't have wasted fifteen minutes of the company's valuable time spinning their wheels with me when they could have been helping other customers. I find that to be typical, by the way: experts serve their customers quickly; non-experts ramble on and tell you things that are inaccurate, untrue, or irrelevant. Make sure the people who answer the phone or work the help desk are not the ones who really need help.

That kind of incident is a reflection of bad training on the part of management. Contrast that with the good training that led to the kind of experience I had at my local Verizon store when I was having problems with my wireless MiFi device. Someone greeted me within sixty seconds of my entering the store. He asked me a couple of questions, immediately diagnosed the problem, downloaded a new program, and sent me on my way with a device that worked, all in under five minutes.

In my experience, companies with excellent service reputations are constantly training and developing every employee from day one until day of departure. They instill the necessary expertise and refresh it constantly, whether through regular newsletters, e-mail, courses, seminars, or retreats. They also encourage and foster the kinds of interactions with fellow managers and employees that lead to the sharing of new tips and tricks. Basically, the organizations with the best service are ones that become environments of continuous learning, at every level of the company. Disney World does all this and more; it has professionally staffed Learning Centers, fully stocked with books, videos, and online courses, that are open to all employees at all times.

Another thing managers can do to constantly refresh learning is to meet regularly with employees and ask what kinds of questions and complaints they receive from customers. Then make sure everyone gets the answers, solutions, and skills they need to deal with those problems, so they are well prepared the next time they crop up.

Ongoing training is a way to ensure not just quality, but consistency of service. This is key, because if people in the company aren't on the same page, your business will suffer. An acquaintance once shared a story that illustrates this perfectly. She was spending a weekend at a hotel. On Saturday, she asked the front desk agent about the cost and duration of the taxi ride to the airport on Monday morning. He said it would take forty-five to ninety minutes, depending on traffic, and cost about $40. On Monday morning, she asked the concierge to get her a taxi. He told her the ride would take less than half an hour and cost about $65. Two employees, two vastly different estimates. Each one was right about one thing and wrong about the other. My acquaintance ended up $25 richer, but with an hour's less sleep and an extra hour on her hands at the airport.

She was not happy about it. The point is, make sure all your employees have the same information and that the information is accurate.

If your manager is not expert enough to help you become an expert, take matters into your own hands. Don't blame your supervisor or your company if you do not have the knowledge and skills you ought to have. Yes, it's their responsibility to train you, but it's also *your* responsibility to develop your skill set and get what you need to do your job with excellence, one way or another. If your manager can't answer your questions, find someone who can. Take advantage of every available resource, within the company and elsewhere. Becoming an expert will not only improve the service you provide to your customers (and in turn help improve your company's bottom line); it will also improve your self-confidence and self-esteem and give you a competitive edge in the job market. Becoming a service expert won't serve just your customers; it will serve *you* well throughout your career and your life.

Rule #12

Rehearse, Rehearse, Rehearse

So we've talked about how great service requires a great script. But even if your script is superb, would you send your cast onstage before a live audience if they were not completely ready to perform at their best? Of course not. To get them ready to put on a great show, you would rehearse, and rehearse, and rehearse again . . . and again. In rehearsals, you discover the flaws in the script and figure out ways to make a good script even better. Sports teams do this, too, of course. They practice and practice and practice some more, and they keep on practicing until the final whistle of the season blows. As your mom always said, "Practice makes perfect."

Why should business be any different? Think about the last time you had to give a presentation at work. Did you go in "cold," or did you run through it at home the night before? In the hospitality industry, it's common for everyone from cocktail server to concierge to go through on-site practice sessions before a restaurant or a hotel opens. Whatever business you're in, you too can benefit from rehearsing. Rehearsals don't cost anything except time, and they pay huge dividends once the curtain goes up.

One simple but excellent form of rehearsal is role-playing. Just assign some employees the role of clients or customers and have others perform their usual jobs. Direct the "customers" to put the employees through their paces by asking tough questions and making difficult demands. Think of scenarios that force the employees to use all their skills. Observe everything they do and say, then follow up with both private feedback and on-the-spot critiques by the whole team. If circumstances permit, you might even want to do what athletic coaches do: shoot videos of the rehearsal and screen them with the team.

Some people may feel uncomfortable performing role-modeling exercises in front of their co-workers and their boss. All the more reason to do it. Anyone who is too self-conscious, or is afraid to look bad to their colleagues, is not quite ready for prime time. Ask successful theater directors, and they will tell you that rehearsing is also the best cure for stage fright. Here's another antidote: Make sure to give everyone *positive* feedback during rehearsals. Don't just single out their mistakes; praise them when they get it right.

If those providing the service are not on-site or are scattered in far-flung locations, not to worry: you can actually role-play using computer simulations. At Disney World, for instance, the safari drivers at Animal Kingdom used to rehearse their spiels while actually driving the safari vehicles out on the savanna. But we soon discovered that using real vehicles in that way was both time-consuming and costly. So now the drivers use computer simulation, much as pilots do. It's not only safer and less expensive, it has the added bonus of allowing them to rehearse at any time.

In addition to teaching employees how to do their jobs under ordinary conditions, rehearsal can prepare them for difficult and unusual situations. That's why I highly recommend bringing all your employees together to list the customer service issues they've encountered most frequently. When that's done, make a list of all the difficulties the employees can *imagine*. Then, as a group, decide how each situation should be handled. You'll never think of everything, but you should be able to anticipate most potential challenges. When you've completed this process, you can use the results to create new rehearsal scenarios. By walking through the most effective responses, you'll be able to solve service problems quickly and keep them from metastasizing. Plus, once rehearsal has made ordinary performance second nature, employees have more mental capacity available for problem solving, so that if a truly novel situation arises, they'll be able to come up with a better solution faster.

Remember, it's not a question of *if* something will

go wrong, it's just a matter of *when*. As Shakespeare said, "The readiness is all." Rehearsals are a great way to make sure everyone is ready to roll when the curtain goes up. It sure makes better sense than practicing on your customers!

Rule #13

Expect More to Get More

Your customers expect a lot from you. To meet those high expectations, you in turn expect a lot from your colleagues and employees. People tend to give what they're expected to give—so expect the best from everyone, and you shall receive it. You might even get *more* than you expected.

One company that gives more to their customers by expecting more from their employees is Stihl, the top-rated maker of power tools. Through my consulting work, I have met many of Stihl's employees, from those in the head office to those on the floor of the manufacturing plant, and I've found they all have one thing in common: they expect excellence and will settle for nothing less. If the slightest thing is wrong with any of their products, that item does not leave the factory until it is reworked to perfection. They expect the best not only from their chain saws and leaf blowers, but also from their people—even their guest speakers. I know this because Stihl once hired me to give a talk to their executive team. Long before the event, their head of marketing, Ken Waldron, invited me to Virginia Beach to see their operation and meet some of their people; he wanted to make sure I understood the company's vision and strategy before I gave my speech. After giving me a tour of the entire facility, he spent a full hour giving me more background on the company and later followed up with an e-mail reviewing everything we had discussed. He even attended one of my other presentations so he could give me feedback on which points were most relevant to Stihl. Ken could not have been clearer about his high expectations for my talk, nor could he have done more to communicate them to me.

That attitude of high expectation should be present everywhere in the organization. Top executives should expect more from management, and management should expect more from staff. In turn, the staff should expect more from their managers, and managers should expect more from the big brass. Most important, everyone should expect more from themselves.

Mind you, setting high expectations will not cost your company one single cent. It does take time and energy, though, because it's not enough just to set these expectations, you have to communicate them—with candor, clarity, and not a shred of ambiguity. Don't just assume your employees or team members know what's expected of them. Tell them. And tell them again. Tell them in every way you can dream up, from memos, to posters on the bulletin board, to e-mails, to tweets, to one-on-one conversations. Leave no room for misunderstanding or contradiction. Consistency is vital. If you don't make your high expectations clear, you will *still* get consistent performance, only it will be consistently average or consistently poor.

You might consider creating a detailed document that explains exactly what you expect from your employees. Distribute it to everyone at every level. Never mind that parts of it do not apply to certain people; they might apply to them in the future as employees change positions. More important, everyone will know what is expected of everyone else. After distributing the document, follow up. Make sure every question is answered and all ambiguities are cleared up.

And be sure to include what they can expect from *you*. When I was running operations at Disney World, I sent a six-page letter to my leadership team titled "Lee's Operating Practices and Priorities: What You Can Expect from Me, and What I Expect from You." Among other things, I wrote: "I am available to talk to you 24 hours a day. Use the following means to contact me depending on the importance and urgency of the message [I added all my phone numbers]. I will make myself equally accessible to people who report directly to me and those who do not. I intend to talk with your employees and managers, probe to find out what is happening in the operation, and try to find areas that warrant my leadership focus. . . . I will keep you informed. If you are not getting the information from me that you need on a timely basis, please tell me. As the amount of communication we receive can be very high volume I try to filter as much as possible. If I filter too much, let me know. . . ."

Even if you're not the boss, you can still set high expectations for those who work with you. Work with your team or department to set goals together and find the best ways to meet them. Constantly challenge your colleagues; push them to do better. A little friendly competition among the ranks doesn't hurt, either; in fact, it can be incredibly motivating. No matter who you are or what your position, if you have big goals, big things can happen.

Bottom line: Your customers hold you to a high standard. If you want to achieve true excellence, raise that bar even higher for yourself, your colleagues, and everyone around you.

Rule #14

Treat Customers the Way
You'd Treat Your Loved Ones

In a way, your customers are like your family; without their loyalty and trust, the road ahead for your business would be rocky indeed. That's why you should treat customers the way you would want your mother and father, spouse and children, and other loved ones to be treated.

Many organizations designate certain customers as VIPs, a status that entitles them to special perks and attention. I would argue that every customer should be a VIP; but when I say VIP, I don't mean "very important person." I mean "very individual person." Just as everyone in your family has his or her unique personality, so is each of your customers an individual, with individual wants and needs. If you're a parent, you probably want each of your children to grow up feeling as if he or she is the most important person in the world. Why not try to make each of your customers feel this way as well?

Think about how you'd want your mom and dad to be treated when they need service. Would you want them to be served at a restaurant by an incompetent waiter with a rotten attitude? Would you want them to be frustrated because the bank teller "helping" them can't answer their questions or give them accurate information? Would you want them to be kept on hold for ten minutes and be forced to listen to bad music or obnoxious ads? Would you want them to be treated by a complacent nurse or doctor? Those are the kinds of questions you and everyone else in your company should be asking yourselves every day. You might think Customer A is a jerk. Customer B might make your blood boil. You might want to throw a package at Customer C instead of gift wrapping it. (Just as we sometimes feel frustrated or infuriated by people in our own families, it's normal to sometimes get aggravated by our customers.) None of it matters. Make each of them feel special anyway—not because it's noble, but because your career and your company will benefit from it.

Once, when Priscilla and I were staying at the City Loft Hotel in Beaufort, South Carolina, I got up early and went to the little coffee shop connected to the hotel. I was greeted cheerfully by a young woman with a very apt name: Joy. "Good morning, how can I serve you?" asked Joy. I told her I would like a blueberry muffin and a cup of coffee. "Can I heat that for you?" she inquired.

"Heat what?" I asked.

"Your muffin," said Joy. "They're better when they're heated."

Now, most servers would throw your muffin in a bag and slam it on the counter, especially before six a.m., when people tend to be grumpy. As country music singer-songwriter Brad Paisley sings in a song called "The World": "To the waiter at the restaurant / You're just another tip." Curious to know what made Joy different, I asked her why she bothered offering to heat the muffin for me. "I always think about what my mother would want if she was the customer," she said.

Bingo! If you think like Joy, you're way ahead of the service game. I had breakfast in that little place every morning for the rest of my trip, because Joy was a joy to see. And I have no doubt that other customers also make it a point to return to the City Loft Hotel and that coffee shop.

The rest of that Brad Paisley song has other examples you don't want to emulate, like the bank teller who treats you as just another account and the beauty shop to whom you're just another head of hair. Instead, you want your customers to feel what Paisley tells the girl he's singing to: "You are the world."

In a way, all the Customer Rules involve making your clientele feel like "the world" by treating them the way you want your loved ones treated. So here I want to focus on two specific parts of the customer experience, the beginning and the end. I learned how crucial those two moments are from my wife and her mother, who once told me how much they appreciate being treated well when they first walk in the door and then again when they leave the premises. It makes sense that first and last impressions have a tremendous influence on a customer's *lasting* impression. A cheery hello and a sincere good-bye can leave a customer with a memory of a positive experience, regardless of what happens in between.

The employees at my branch of the SunTrust Bank are expert at making customers feel special when they enter and when they depart. Lela Johnson, the branch manager, sets the tone by example. Whenever I walk into the bank, she steps out of her office to say hello and ask how Priscilla is doing. And if she sees me on my way out, she always takes the time to say good-bye. That hospitality does not increase the interest the bank pays me on my deposits, but it does increase my interest in doing business with SunTrust.

So I encourage people in all businesses, not just stores or hotels or restaurants, but any outfit—whether it's a law firm or a financial services provider or a corporate headquarters—to place a friendly, outgoing employee at or near the entrance. Don't keep customers waiting; in this high-speed era they want to be served quickly. And here's an added benefit if you work in a retail outlet: It has been proven that when an employee looks customers in the eye and speaks to them, shoplifting goes down dramatically. That alone might cover the cost of having an employee at the door.

And don't forget to conclude the interaction in a way that encourages a return visit. Whether or not your customer or client made a purchase, or closed a deal, or signed on the dotted line, make sure to walk him to the door and thank him for coming. Show that you're grateful she stopped by and let her know that you hope she'll return again and again.

By the same token, if you're a manager and you want your employees or direct reports to treat your customers the way they would their loved ones, you need to make sure you treat *them* the way you would your customers. Think of this as the Golden Rule of customer service: Do unto your employees as you would have them do unto your customers. Customers don't want just a good product; they also want to feel valued, they want to be respected as individuals, and they want authentic human connection. Well, that's what your employees want, too. And if you give it to them, they'll pass it along to those they serve.

This simple, straightforward principle applies to every employee in your organization, including all those who work behind the scenes and never see a customer. These are the people who make sure everything works properly and all the materials you need to run your business are well maintained and easy to find. They keep the facilities clean. They're responsible for forecasting, and purchasing supplies, and keeping the communication technology humming and up-to-date. They load and unload the trucks and stock the storerooms and shelves. Whatever they do, those employees matter, because all of their tasks affect the level of service the customer receives. Think of them as the backstage crew at a theater; without them the actors onstage cannot do their jobs.

I use the acronym ARE to describe what employees want from management: appreciation, recognition, and encouragement. ARE is like a cost-free, infinitely renewable fuel. It never runs out, no matter how much of it you use, and the more of it you give to your employees, the more they will have in reserve to give to your customers. If you master the habit of showering your employees with ARE, you will see rapid improvement in both employee satisfaction and customer satisfaction. So make sure every manager in your organization dispenses ARE generously. If your managers don't know how to do this, teach them; if they prove unteachable, recast them in another role or get rid of them. Any manager who can't give out ARE is bad for business.

Early in my career, I was considered a good manager because I knew how to get things done. But I did not know how to treat the people under me, and that shortcoming was not only holding me back, it was holding my employees back from delivering the excellent service our customers expected and deserved. Fortunately, I woke up to this deficiency and learned about the importance of giving them more ARE. In short order, it trickled down to our customers.

When people are made to feel that they matter, they develop self-confidence and self-esteem, and that translates to good performance. Employees who are *not* treated as if they matter perform as if their jobs don't matter, either. This is human nature, just as people who don't feel loved find it hard to *give* love. So if you want your customers to feel they're important, make sure your employees feel important, too. I saw a sterling example of this not long ago, when Priscilla and I had lunch at the Pentagon with General Lloyd Austin, the army's vice chief of staff. When we finished lunch, General Austin excused himself to walk over to the dining room server and thank him for his attentive service. Then he went into the kitchen to thank the cooks for preparing such a nice lunch. If a four-star general has time to deliver ARE to people who can do nothing to advance his own career, I'm sure that you do, too. Learn what makes your employees feel significant and valued and then give it to them.

Wouldn't you want your mom to be treated this way?

Rule #15

Be Like a Bee

When I give speeches and workshops, I'm usually introduced as the man who ran Disney World operations for ten years. Then the person introducing me talks about how I oversaw the forty thousand cast members (employees) responsible for keeping Disney World's numerous hotels, theme parks, golf courses, shopping and entertainment centers, and sports complex humming. Inevitably, I'm then asked, "How did you keep track of everything?" The fact of the matter is that I had no idea what was going on in each and every corner of that vast enterprise—how could I? What I did know, at all times, was this: I could trust the many highly competent people who reported to me to know exactly what was going on in their areas of responsibility. My job was not to know every single thing that was happening; it was to buzz around helping every one of those executives, managers, and frontline people perform just a little better every day.

In doing so, I took inspiration from the following story about the company's founder. A little girl visiting Disneyland once asked Walt Disney if he still drew Mickey Mouse. Walt replied that he no longer drew the characters he created.

"Do you still write stories?" she asked.

Walt said, "No, I don't write stories anymore, either."

"Then what do you do?" asked the perplexed girl.

Walt paused for a moment, then explained: "I'm like a bee that flits from flower to flower, taking a little pollen here and a little pollen there, and I build up all the honey in the honeycomb." He meant that he buzzed around the Disney facilities, pollinating the imagination of every employee to help them become more creative and more productive.

This is a good rule for managers who want to improve customer service in their team, department, or company. If you want your business to thrive in a competitive environment, you need to make sure things are constantly improving, day in and day out. I learned early in my career that you can improve only some things by yourself, but you can move mountains if you spread that positive intention to everyone in your domain. Military people call this a "force multiplier"; Walt Disney used the phrase "plus it up." Whatever you call it, imagine what great service you could deliver if everyone in your beehive was in the habit of gathering and spreading good ideas to improve performance.

Just as nature is doomed without busy bees pollinating the flowers, organizations are doomed without leaders who pollinate the minds of their employees and without employees who pollinate the minds of their colleagues. But there's one difference: For bees, pollinating is a seasonal job; for those who want to constantly improve the service their teams or employees deliver, it's a daily responsibility. They have to wake up every morning ready to pollinate. The longer I spent in executive positions, the more I came to think that my main responsibility was to connect with as many employees as I could and offer up as many ideas as possible about how to make things better. Sometimes my suggestions were spot-on; other times they were way off the mark. But either way, the conversation stimulated fresh thinking, promoted questioning, and inspired everyone around me to come up with better ways to do things.

As you buzz around your organization, don't just tell people what's wrong with the status quo. Faultfinding is unhelpful if your aim is to spread the habit of creative thinking. Instead, focus on how things might be better. But don't just flat-out tell people how to improve things. Instead, *ask*. Those on the front lines delivering service will come up with better ideas than you can if you give them the freedom to think and express themselves without fear.

When I got to Disney World, I had a lot of experience in the hospitality industry but zero experience in theme parks, outside of visiting a couple with my family. So I asked lots of questions that must have seemed dumb to the people working for me. But this turned out to be a blessing. I didn't get stuck in the rut of "This is how it's done," because I *didn't know* how it was done. And my ignorance gave those who *did* know the confidence and courage to offer up ideas.

This is a useful strategy for any manager to adopt, no matter how much experience you have and no matter how much know-how you've acquired over the course of your career. Expertise is a great and valuable thing, but it can also stifle innovative thinking. "Because it's always been done that way" is about the worst answer possible to the question "Why do we do it that way?"

I admit that not everyone appreciated having me buzz around their areas, asking how we could improve things. But I was persistent, and eventually I wore down the resistance with my enthusiasm and my sincere respect for the employees' expertise. Here are some of the questions I would ask people when I dropped by to pollinate their work areas. I highly recommend that you adapt them as appropriate to your business and job responsibilities.

* Why do you do it this way?
* Do you think there's a better way?

- ✳ Have you ever thought of doing it this way instead?
- ✳ What do your customers like most about the way things are done?
- ✳ What do they *not* like?
- ✳ What do you hate having to say to customers?
- ✳ If you could change two things about the way we currently serve customers, what would they be?

You might also come with a prepared list of questions specific to each area. For example:

- ✳ What is the average customer waiting time at peak hours?
- ✳ What items do you frequently run out of?
- ✳ How many customers do you serve in an average morning, as compared with the afternoon?
- ✳ Is there any way we can increase those numbers?
- ✳ How many of those customers leave satisfied?
- ✳ What percentage of the customers you see are one-timers, and what percentage return repeatedly?
- ✳ How can we use your time productively when business is light?

Questions like these may never get asked unless you ask them, and every one of them—and countless others—can lead to creative ways to make things better.

The more you learn, the more ideas you'll have. And this kind of inquiry costs nothing but time, and it will pay off in employee confidence and initiative.

You might also "plus it up" by bringing all the bees together from time to time to reload their imaginations. Schedule regular idea-sharing sessions, perhaps weekly or monthly. Some of the ideas you generate might not be relevant at that time or not yet fleshed out enough to be practical. Write down anything that might be remotely useful and put the collection of ideas in a file. You never know what will prove valuable later on. Sometimes the best solutions arise when seemingly unrelated ideas come together in unexpected ways.

Remember, whatever your position in the company, you are both the bee and the flower. Both roles are vital, and they are intertwined. The more you allow yourself to be pollinated, the better you'll be at pollinating others. Even if you're *not* a manager, you can pollinate your workplace with inspiration and ideas. No matter your role or title, if you want to provide better customer service, start buzzing around looking for better ways to do things. Remember, it is never too late to get better.

Rule #16

Know the Truth, the Whole Truth, and Nothing but the Truth

lbert Einstein once said, "Whoever is careless with the truth in small matters cannot be trusted with important matters." No matter what company you work for or what exactly you do, you are engaged in the very important matter of serving your customers to the best of your ability. When it comes to service, no truth is too small to be careless about.

If you do not know the truth about what your customers need and want, think and feel, you will not make the right decisions about serving them. What could be more obvious? Yet many organizations fail to make a priority of seeking out the truth. They prefer to spend their days in willful ignorance, basking in the (false) conviction that they know everything there is to know about their customers. Finding the truth is not always comfortable, because it can have sharp edges.

But if you don't know about those sharp edges, they will cut you when you least expect it. You'll see the blood on the bottom line when your customers run for the hills.

One reason you have to dig for the truth, rather than expect it to come to you, is that people don't like to rock the boat. True, some customers are quick to complain when they are unsatisfied; these are the ones who stand out. But what about all the ones who *don't* complain because they're too timid or simply because they are nice people who don't want to get anyone in trouble? In fact, most customers would prefer to settle for less-than-perfect service rather than get into a confrontation or spend their valuable time hassling, and they won't make the truth known unless something really egregious or costly occurs. I have to admit that I'm that way myself. When an employee of a business asks me how everything was, more often than not I say, "Everything was fine," even if it wasn't. In some cases, I just don't have the time or energy to explain what was wrong. In other instances, I've already made up my mind not to do business with that company again, so I figure, why bother? This is why you need to put in that extra effort to uncover how customers *really* feel about the service they receive from you.

Oscar Wilde once said that "the pure and simple truth is rarely pure and never simple." I interpret this to mean one should never settle for easy answers and never let mere facts pass for the truth. That's why I work harder to discern the reality beneath the facts, whether it's in regard to my personal relationships, public affairs, or business. That's a good route to follow when it comes to customer service, too. The real truth is what the customers genuinely feel, not what you or your employees *think* they feel. As I tell everyone in my speeches, "Don't believe everything you think. At least half of it is probably not true."

I once saw another quote that stuck in my mind: "I shouldn't have eavesdropped, but sometimes that's the only way to find out the truth." I'll admit it, over the course of my career I eavesdropped on customers a lot. I got into the habit when I was waiting tables, back at the beginning of my career. Once I realized how much I could learn about the people at my tables by listening to their chatter (it's amazing what diners will say in front of a waiter), I was able to bring them things I heard they wanted and fix the things I heard them complain about. Plus, because eavesdropping helped me understand them better, I was able to deliver those little things they didn't even *know* they wanted but that ended up making the experience more pleasurable for them. After a while, I noticed I was getting above average tips and that many guests were asking to be seated at my table when they returned. I never forgot that.

Having learned the value of knowing the truth, I kept eavesdropping even when I was an executive running huge operations. I would wander anonymously through the lobbies of the hotels I was managing or the dining rooms of the restaurants I was overseeing, like a spy, just watching and listening. In fact, even now that my corporate days are over, I still eavesdrop, because I learn a lot that way. I do it so much that Priscilla often scolds me for being so obvious about it.

Of course, there are other ways to learn the truth besides spying on your customers—first and foremost being to simply ask them directly! I believe that every employee who comes into contact with customers should be trained to ask questions designed to get at the truth. These might include the following:

* Did you find everything you were looking for?
* Is there anything else I can do for you today?
* What can we do better?
* What do we do that you don't particularly like?
* Is there anything else we could have done to make your time with us better?
* What do we do well that keeps you coming back?
* Would you recommend us to your best friend and loved ones? If yes, why? If no, why not?

In addition, every business should keep a log of customer complaints. And don't discount the power of the traditional survey. These days, you can use everything from smartphone apps to live Internet chats to find out what customers really think about you. But always remember to dig deeper, listen harder, and never settle for the first thing you hear. Your customers will translate the queries as "These people really care."

As the Buddha said, "Three things cannot be long hidden: the sun, the moon, and the truth." Just like the sun and the moon, the truth will reveal itself in time. If your customers don't tell you the hard truth, they'll tell it to their friends—including all their Facebook friends—and that could be the beginning of the end for your business. Don't let the truth reveal itself on your customers' Facebook pages or Twitter feeds. Instead, make sure it's revealed to you. The truth is golden, and each customer is a goose that lays golden eggs.

Rule #17

Listen Up

When I worked for Marriott, in one of my annual performance reviews my boss, Karl Kilburg, suggested I take a course to improve my listening skills. "You often don't listen to what I'm saying to you," he said.

I immediately became defensive and tried to tell him why he was wrong. In doing so, I proved his point: I heard his words, but I hadn't really *listened*. I didn't ask him to elaborate or explain. I just sprang to my own defense. Later, after I calmed down, I thought about the many times Priscilla had accused me of not listening to her. Naturally, she said it in a different way and in a different tone of voice, usually, "Lee, are you listening to me?" Needless to say, that was not really a question. I realized that Karl was right: I had a lot to learn about listening.

If your customers don't feel they're being listened

to, they will not be as straightforward as Priscilla and Karl. They'll just return the favor by not listening to you when invited back to do more business with you. That's why I recommend making sure every employee who's in contact with customers or clients masters the art of listening. Eventually, I listened to Karl and signed up for a three-day course that Marriott's human resources department found for me. It turned out to be one of the best things I ever did to improve my management and leadership skills. It helped at home, too, although I have to confess that I'm not always perfect. Just the other day, Priscilla insisted that I go to the doctor to get my hearing checked. When I got home, I told her the test results: "My hearing is fine." She said, "Then we have a bigger problem." *That*, I heard loud and clear.

Failing to truly listen to others is just a bad habit, and it's one most of us have to some degree. It's all too easy to talk too much and listen much too little. Luckily, habits can be changed. Sure it takes time and effort, but it pays off in customer satisfaction.

Like all of us, your customers want to be understood. But emotionally, what's even more important is that they feel you *want* to understand them and you're genuinely *trying* to grasp what they want, need, think, and feel. They may forgive you for not comprehending, but they won't ever forgive you for not caring. And they judge how much you care by how well you listen.

I had a disappointing experience recently with a young employee at a popular burger joint near my home. I wanted to place a takeout order, but I had to call four times before someone finally answered the phone. It was not the first time I'd had a problem ordering takeout from that restaurant, so when I arrived to pick up the burgers, I tried politely to tell the young server what had happened. Instead of listening to my very legitimate complaint, he immediately became arrogant and defensive, saying that company policy was to serve the customers in the restaurant before the ones calling for takeout and the restaurant was very busy that night. I found this difficult to swallow, so I wrote a letter to the CEO. I promptly got a call from the district manager, who confirmed my suspicion: it was *not* their policy to handle customers in the store before answering the phone. The employee had invented an excuse just to shut me up.

Clearly this employee did *not* understand service. He not only didn't care about my problem, he didn't realize that it was also *his* problem. I can't be sure if he suffered any consequences because I spoke to his manager, but if he had simply paid attention to me and demonstrated a modicum of concern, I would have let it go without saying a word.

It's funny how much more effort we put into developing our speaking skills than we do into improving our listening abilities. When I was in college I took a speech course. I knew that speaking well would be an important skill to have when I entered the working world. I also knew that public speaking terrifies most people and that if I could somehow rise above that common fear, I would have a leg up. The day before I was scheduled to give a speech to the class, I got so scared that I dropped the course. The thought of being observed and judged was more than I could handle. Today I give speeches for a living. How did I overcome my fear? I was lucky enough to get great advice from a speech professor and smart enough to practice the techniques he taught me.

Mastering the art of listening should be just as straightforward. There are techniques for getting better at it, but very few people take advantage of them, because we seldom appreciate how important listening is. Plus, most of us believe we're already good at it—or at least good at faking it. The truth is, most of us in this hectic world are *not* good at listening. And no matter how good we think we are at faking it, 99 percent of the time we're not fooling anybody but ourselves.

Here are some tips for practicing the art of listening:

* Get into the right position to listen. By that I mean speak to the customer in a quiet location where you will not be distracted.
* Give the customer your full attention. Maintain eye contact. Don't interrupt. Don't multitask. Don't show any signs of impatience or distraction with your body language.
* Don't try to anticipate what the customer is going to say; you are not a mind reader.

* If possible, take notes. Don't count on remembering everything that was said.
* Give the speaker a chance to finish before you reply. You might even ask, "Is there anything else you would like to tell me?" before responding.
* When the customer is finished speaking, reiterate or paraphrase what he or she said. For example, "I think you are saying that the blender you purchased from us stopped working on certain settings and you would like us to replace it even though it's been more than thirty days since you bought it." You may not remember all the details, especially if the person is angry or long-winded (or both), but rephrasing will ensure that you clearly understand the main points.
* Once you verify what was said, ask additional questions to improve your understanding.
* At every step, make the customer feel valued and appreciated.
* And for goodness' sake, if you receive a complaint, apologize. Saying you're sorry can be the best way to make customers feel that you care. (See Rule #36, "Apologize Like You Really Mean It.")

But it doesn't end there. Great listening means paying attention not only to what people say, but also to what they *don't* say and to what they're *trying* to say but can't quite articulate. To do that, you have to be as focused as a laser beam. Sometimes customers are unhappy with some aspect of your products or services and don't know how to explain their concerns. Some don't really know what they want, while others know exactly what they are looking for but can't quite describe it. And in some cases they are reticent because they fear embarrassment—as with people who need tech support and are too self-conscious to admit that they're intimidated by technology, or people who have medical needs related to an intimate condition. Whatever the reason, an attentive listener can tell when the customer is either holding back information or struggling to find the right words. I have found that the best way to work with such people is to ask questions and listen carefully to the answers.

Your probe should be conducted with the utmost diplomacy—politely, patiently, and gently. Ask the customer if there is anything else he would like to tell you that will help you understand and serve him better. Let her know that you really do want to hear everything she has to say and that no concern is too trivial and no question is foolish. Make it safe for customers to disclose what is really on their minds. If you put them at ease and ask the right questions, you will eventually achieve clarity about what they need and want, whether it's a product, a service, constructive advice, or a fair redress of a grievance.

As Stephen Covey said in his bestselling book, *The*

7 Habits of Highly Effective People, "Seek first to understand, then to be understood." He recognized that customers who feel understood are likely to come back and those who *don't* feel understood will go where the employees have better ears.

Rule #18

Be a Copycat

Have you ever noticed that some of the most successful companies got where they are by taking a great idea from another company and improving upon it? For example, Apple made history when it introduced the mouse to computer users. Apple didn't invent the mouse; IBM engineers did. But it was Steve Jobs who saw the potential of the technology, adapted it to Apple's personal computer design, and then proceeded to blow the minds of consumers—and revolutionize the world of personal computing at the same time.

You can improve your company's or department's customer service in much the same way, by soaking up ideas like a sponge and adapting them for your purposes. You might copy an innovative procedure, or a creative policy, or even just a handy phrase that puts customers at ease. You might even copy something indirectly related to service, like a training program, or a technological upgrade, or the layout of a retail or work space. But the best copycats don't just imitate; they pay attention to everything around them, spot the best ideas, and then find a better way to apply them.

Despite what your third-grade teacher might have told you, copying is not cheating, at least when it comes to business. Unless what you are copying is trademarked or legally protected in some way, there is no law against taking another business's idea and adapting it to your needs; if there were, some of the best innovations on the planet would never have come to be. In fact, *not* being a copycat is cheating—it's cheating yourself. Think about it this way: As soon as one of your competitors installs a better service system or invents a faster way of doing things, they'll eventually start stealing *your* customers, and before long you'll be wishing you'd copied them when you had the opportunity. So stay closely tuned to everything your competitors are doing, and don't hesitate to take their best practices and run with them.

The hotel industry is a great example of one that thrives on copycatting. Every major hotel chain now has express check-in, express checkout, preorder breakfast menus, flat-screen TVs, exercise rooms, frequent-traveler awards programs, and other new amenities. If you remove the company's name and logo, you can usher a frequent traveler into any major hotel chain and chances are she won't even be able to tell which one she's in. Each of those innovations started somewhere, and now they're everywhere, with the chains racing to improve their versions before the others do. Nowadays, no hotel dares *not* to copy and build on a good idea, and the beneficiaries are the travelers, who need a comfortable place to rest their heads.

When I realized the importance of copycatting, I trained myself to observe carefully and make notes about everything I saw that might improve my personal or business life. To this day, when I go to a hotel, a restaurant, a bank, an airport, a doctor's office, a shopping mall, or anywhere else, I file away things I see, then think about how I can implement them in my life or relate them to my audiences when I give speeches. For example, not long ago Priscilla and I took a vacation trip to Vietnam. Because we won the package at a charity auction to benefit cancer research, we stayed at the Six Senses Resorts & Spas. The service was spectacular. But the one thing that really grabbed my attention was the pillows. They actually offered *sixteen* different pillow selections, of every shape and size and filled with everything from foam to feathers to pecan shells. Guests even had a choice of aromatherapy scents for their pillows, to help them sleep better. I have never seen offerings like those in any other hotel, and my work has taken me to hundreds of them. If I still worked in the hospitality business, I'd have started copycatting those pillow ideas the second I got off the plane. As it is, I have used the experience to remind companies in every industry to always look for new ways to impress their customers.

One last thing to remember: You don't have to

confine yourself to direct competitors when looking for things to copycat. Smart people look *outside* their industry for great ideas and tweak them for their own purposes. Whatever business you're in, you can learn from excellence wherever you find it.

Here are some suggestions for how to go about harvesting ideas:

* Go to a mall and visit as many stores as you can, writing down every good customer service practice you observe. When you get back to your office, look over that list and think about how the best practices can be applied to your business.
* Give your employees or colleagues the challenge to share all the good service-related practices they come across as they go about their daily lives. Offer a prize to the five best ideas that can be implemented in your business.
* Find out who's the best at doing what you would like to do better, and study them. Pay them a visit. Speak to their employees and their clientele. See what online chat groups are saying about them.
* Stay informed about your industry by reading trade magazines, attending conferences, and Googling everything you can think of. There is no substitute for firsthand experience, but there is something to be said for leaving no stone unturned.

* Cultivate professional relationships. Having a network of colleagues is like being enrolled in a lifelong learning institute with a top-notch faculty. Pick your associates' brains for ideas, and don't hesitate to share your wisdom with them so they owe you one.
* Read, read, and read some more. Read books, magazines, Internet articles, the daily newspaper. Look for ideas in every story and in every ad.
* Hang out with smart people in all types of businesses. Get them to talk about how they do what they do. It's virtually certain that they'll know things you don't know but should know.

Imitation is not only the sincerest form of flattery, it's a smart way to get better at what you do, especially if you can creatively adapt what you learn to maximize results. Remember, you don't have to be the first or the biggest; you only have to be the best. And one of the keys to being the best is to keep your eyes, ears, and mind open all the time. Ideas are free, so cast your net wide and snatch them up wherever you find them. Once you've hauled in a great one, think about how you can do it cheaper, better, or faster.

If you still doubt the wisdom of copycatting, think about this the next time you order your favorite coffee drink. Many years ago, while attending a trade show in Italy, Howard Schultz discovered the small espresso bars scattered throughout Milan and Verona. He watched in awe as the baristas ground the beans, pulled the shots of espresso, foamed the milk, and served up a hot, steaming beverage unlike any he'd ever seen. What he did next is now business history. He took what he saw, improved upon the idea, and implemented it as Starbucks. In 2011, Schultz was named *Fortune* magazine's Businessperson of the Year. To me, he's one of the greatest copycats in business history.

Rule #19

Fish Where the Fishermen Ain't

Warren Buffett, America's most admired investor, once said that one simple rule dictates his approach to investing: "Be fearful when others are greedy, and be greedy when others are fearful." This is the flip side of the copycat rule: Look at what others are *not* doing, and seize that opportunity to do it yourself. It's kind of like how in fishing it's sometimes best to cast your line where no one else thinks there are fish.

It's not a question of being different just for the sake of being different. That can get you nowhere quickly. Great businesses stand out by being different from the rest in the *right way*: by finding customer needs that are going unmet and figuring out a way to meet them. One example of a company that has done this successfully is Chick-fil-A. When S. Truett Cathy founded Chick-fil-A, it didn't take him long to figure out that every other fast-food chain was serving hamburgers but very few were serving chicken. That's why today, Chick-fil-A serves chicken, chicken, and nothing but chicken. How is that a good business proposition? Think of it this way. If you have a hankering for a burger, you could go to any of a number of fast-food chains competing for your business. But if you are in the mood for chicken, you have fewer choices, and if there's a Chick-fil-A nearby, that's where you're likely to go.

Doing what others don't do has also paid off for Southwest Airlines. For instance, they are one of the few airlines that let customers change flights with no charge—a huge plus for someone who travels a lot and often has to adjust departure dates or times. If you cancel a flight, they give you full credit for up to twelve months. And unlike most other airlines, they don't charge for checking baggage (up to two pieces). But you don't have to be a giant corporation or a national chain to stand out by offering a service no one else does. For example, consider Mollie Stone's Markets in the San Francisco Bay Area. Two of the local chain's nine stores—both located in areas where hills are steep and parking is impossible—offer something called the Mollie Bus, a drop-off service that transports customers and their packages from the store to their homes. It runs regularly, according to demand, and it's free with a purchase of $30 or more. You can imagine how welcome that is to area residents, especially those with physical limitations. It no doubt gives Mollie Stone's a huge advantage in a highly competitive business.

When you're out and about, every time you have a thought such as "Wouldn't it be great if they . . ." or "If only they offered . . . ," write it down, because you might be able to convert that idea into a unique service innovation. And while you're checking out what your competitors are doing, ask yourself not only what you can imitate, but what you can do that's radically different. Is there something that's the opposite of what they do? If they're trying to sell every product under the sun, like Target or Walmart, can you specialize in a single item? If they pride themselves on having lots of store locations, can you consolidate to a single space but offer a super-efficient delivery service? If they take three days to do something, can you do it today? If they're open from nine to five, can you stay open from eight to six? If they charge for shipping, can you ship for free or for a dollar? If their voice mail says they'll get back to you within twenty-four hours, can you answer the phone and take care of customers immediately? If they sell it unassembled, can you sell it fully assembled? You get the picture. The idea is to find out what customers aren't getting from your competitors and give it to them.

In a competitive, fast-changing world, the companies that can satisfy a unique customer need will emerge the winners. If you need any more incentive, just remember the slogan that helped propel Apple from near ruin to the most profitable company in America back in 1997: "Think Different."

Rule #20

Be a Wordsmith—Language Matters

"Watch your language!" my mother used to say to my brother and me. She was referring to our penchant for using foul language, of course, but as I progressed through my career I learned that her statement carried far greater meaning. When used in certain ways, *lots* of words can be foul and offensive, not just those so-called four-letter ones.

Leadership expert Frances Hesselbein once said, "When is the last time you heard someone say, 'I can't wait to be a subordinate'?" Her point was that the word *subordinate* means inferior, and no one aspires to being inferior, so why not use a more aspirational term when referring to those who report to you? Luckily, many executives have learned this lesson and now use more dignified language like "associates" for their employees. Another term I'd like to see disappear is "my people," as in "My people are doing a great job with customer service." Unless you're a king or a queen, I'd suggest that you refrain from using that phrase. The people who report to you are not "yours," even if you sign their paychecks and have the power to fire them. If you use demeaning language to refer to them, they'll resent it, and that feeling will be reflected in how they serve customers.

These are just two examples of why words matter in business. Words have the power to dispirit or motivate. They can hurt or heal. They can start a war or stop one. Just a few simple words have the power to describe a vision, as in "I have a dream." Words create pictures in our minds for better or for worse, and the words we remember most are those that touch the heart first.

The wrong words can slowly but surely infect an organization's culture like a virus. If demeaning, degrading, or discouraging terms are used habitually, morale plummets and so does service. Then customers start to vanish, one at a time. I remember boarding an Eastern Air Lines flight in Bermuda in the 1980s and overhearing one flight attendant say to another, "Here come the animals." She was referring to the passengers. Eastern went under not too long after that. Apparently, the "animals" had found other airlines to fly, and I wasn't a bit surprised.

The words you use in relation to customers carry tremendous weight. That's why so many companies now call their customers "guests." If you refer to those who use your product or service as your guests, you can bet that your employees—or associates—will treat them accordingly.

The words you use when you speak to—or about— your customers should signal respect and concern, as if each customer were the most important person in the world. Don't forget that certain terms that are perfectly fine to use in your personal life are *not* fine to use with customers. For example, "What do you guys want to eat?" may be appropriate to say to your children or a group of friends watching the Super Bowl, but it's not what a server should say to a couple dining in a nice restaurant. "Guys" is overly familiar, and some customers might take it as sexist.

Here's one of my wife's pet peeves: "There's a Priscilla Cockerell here to see you." "There's a" sounds too much like "There's a spider in the sink" or "There's a mouse in the attic." Listen to the difference between that and "Priscilla Cockerell is here to see you."

In a customer service context, words with an upbeat, can-do connotation can work magic. "Definitely," "surely," "absolutely," "certainly": all winners, and far superior to "maybe."

Here are a few other pointers:

* "How can I help you?" is better than "What can I do for you?"
* "Let me show you where it is" sounds much more helpful than "It's over there."

* "It's my pleasure" is more congenial than "Sure" or "No problem."
* Instead of "That's not my responsibility," try "Let me get someone who knows more about that than I do."

The language that inspires customer confidence and trust is always positive, polite, and respectful. The right words can work wonders, so make sure you use them sincerely.

Make Yourself Available

When Priscilla and I decided to put tile on our deck, it took us forever to pick just the right pattern. On one visit to a tile store, two great things happened. First, the woman running the shop really listened to what we had to say and quickly directed us to what seemed to be the perfect tile. But before we pulled the trigger, we wanted the opinion of our contractor, Wyatt Anderson. So we called him from the shop, and without a moment's hesitation, he said, "Stay there, I'll be right over." He drove there in less than thirty minutes, looked at the tile, and concurred with our choice. "I think this is going to work really well," he said.

Wyatt did something that everyone should do if they want to raise customer satisfaction to astronomical levels: he made himself immediately available. He dropped what he was doing and went the extra mile—actually twenty miles, in his case—to be there for his customers. Now Priscilla and I recommend him to anyone in Orlando who needs a contractor.

It might sound obvious that you should be as available to your customers as humanly possible, but it's amazing how many employees and companies forget this. Haven't you ever been in a store, or at a bank, or at a place like the DMV, where you practically have to hire a detective to get an answer to a question? Haven't you ever sat at a restaurant table and had to do everything short of scream to get a menu or a glass of water? That should never happen, and in establishments that put the customer at the center of their universe it *doesn't* happen, because employees know to always be available.

A saying I once heard sums up this ethos perfectly: "Don't be in the storeroom if there's a customer in the store." This is a good motto for all kinds of organizations and operations. It applies even to online services, if you think about it. If your business is primarily Web-based, there still needs to be someone waiting to pick up the phone if a customer calls with a problem, and there still needs to be someone on hand to do the support if something on the site goes awry.

This doesn't apply just to line staff. Whatever your job title, whatever your status, you're not important enough to seal yourself off. In fact, the greater your authority, the more crucial it is to make yourself visible and available. When an employee comes up against a problem, such as an upset customer or an unusual request that he or she does not have either the knowledge or the authority to handle, someone who *does* have the knowledge and authority must be easy to reach. To a customer, the response "Let me get my manager" can be a major tension reducer. But the tension will return big-time if he or she has to wait . . . and wait . . . and wait some more before that manager shows up. And it might boil over completely if the end result is "I'm sorry, my manager is not available at the moment." What is more important than being immediately available for an anxious customer who needs attention?

Nowadays, with all our smartphones and communication devices, anyone who claims he or she can't be reached is sending the message that he or she does not *want* to be reached. Once, when I didn't take her call, Priscilla asked me, "Who is more important than I am?" There is only one answer to that question—nobody—so I advise you to always take calls from your loved ones. In the business context, your customers are the most important people in the world, so you should strive to be just as available for them as you would be for your spouse. Once I learned that important lesson, wherever I worked I instructed my office staff to interrupt me if I got a call from either a customer or my wife. If you think taking calls from customers is beneath you, you're probably conveying the wrong attitude in other ways as well.

No matter what your position in the company, availability also means being prepared to roll up your sleeves to help take care of customers when the situation calls for it. At companies with reputations for outstanding customer service, managers are always out there getting their hands dirty. One reason Disney World's percentage of return guests is through the roof is their policy of having frontline managers spend 80 percent of their time out in the park. At Southwest and JetBlue, managers even help clean the planes! It doesn't matter if it's not in your job description. It should be. Not only does it make for a happier, more cohesive work environment, but if you're in a position of authority, I guarantee that your cooperative attitude will rub off on everyone. Those who read my last book, *Creating Magic*, will remember that one of my leadership lessons is to be careful what you say and do, because as a leader, you are being watched and judged every second of every day. When your employees see you out among the staff and customers, being available to chip in, they will quickly get the message and emulate your service-driven attitude.

If you're a high-ranking executive at a large company, you may not have the time to get out there and clean planes, and you can't realistically be available to take every single customer phone call. But even if your customers can't reach you 24/7, it's still your responsibility to make sure they have a way to reach *someone* who can help them. They may not get to vent their frustration or make a suggestion directly to you, but they should find it easy to communicate with your organization in a personal way and be heard at a level that really counts. By this I do not mean a generic e-mail form on your website. Put a phone number there instead and have a real live person answer the phone.

Not long ago, I heard an ad on a PBS broadcast that began: "Support for this podcast comes from Allied Bank, committed to customer service, with the option to reach a human being at any time at [phone number] by pressing zero." It says a lot that a major bank would use its precious few seconds of airtime to make the promise that a real person will answer the phone, instead of, say, ". . . where you can get good interest rates," or, ". . . where our mortgage experts are always there to help you." Take a page from their playbook. People like to talk to fellow human beings, so make sure real human beings in your company are available to talk to customers. Whenever I call Smith, Carney & Co., the Oklahoma City firm that has done my taxes for many years, a receptionist promptly answers the phone and connects me to my accountant, Joe Hornick. Recently, I told Joe how much I appreciate hearing a human voice answer the phone. He told me they'd considered installing an automated phone system but decided not to. They realized that anyone can do taxes, so if they wanted to keep their customers, they had better focus on great service. My stockbrokers, Larry Reed, Mara Levitt, and Brian Coatoam with Merrill Lynch, do the same thing: they answer the phone. And as long as they do, I'll continue to not only bring them my business, but recommend them to others.

I also suggest putting a mailing address on your website with your name in it, so customers can write to you. Believe it or not, some people still prefer actual postal mail to e-mail, and since having an address to write to is rare these days, providing one will make your company stand out. When I was at Disney, I received and read more than seven hundred letters a month, and it paid off in customer loyalty and bottom-line results.

Thanks in part to advances in mobile communication, there are dozens of ways to be available these days. Find the ones that make the most sense for your circumstances, and make sure everyone else on your team does the same. If you ever need to contact me, just go to my website, www.LeeCockerell.com. There you will find my address, my e-mail, and my cell phone number. When you call me, I will answer the phone myself.

Rule #22

Always Be the Giving One

In the introduction, I wrote about how my granddaughter, Margot, then twelve, told me that the first
rule of customer service is "Be nice." Well, when I later
mentioned that I was quoting her in this book, Margot's
ten-year-old brother, Tristan, piped up to say that he
wanted to be in my book, too. "Then you better give
me a good quote," I said. "What does service mean to
you?"

Without a second's hesitation, he said, "When you
serve, you should always be the giving one."

Why do children get it so easily while so many
adults don't? To Tristan, it's just common sense that it's
good to be the giving one. He gets satisfaction from
helping others. Ask him to do something for you and
his face lights up. In fact, you might not have to ask.
One of his teachers told my daughter-in-law, Valerie,
that Tristan saw her carrying an armful of packages to

her car one day and rushed over to ask if he could help. In our me-centered world, wouldn't it be nice if everyone who served us was like Tristan?

If you ask a few average managers or even CEOs what service means, they're likely to go on about the services and amenities their companies offer: "We're open twenty-four hours a day." "We offer free home delivery." "We have leather seats for preferred customers." Those are services, not service. Service is when people give of their time, their energy, and their compassion, with little or no expectation of receiving equal value in return. In my opinion, there are plenty of services in the business world; what we need is more service from people who like to be the giving ones.

I saw genuine givers up front and personal a few years ago when Priscilla became so ill that she almost died. She's doing great now, thanks in large part to the nurses and other hospital personnel at Orlando Health, and especially to her surgeon, Dr. Paul Williamson. Dr. Williamson is considered the best colorectal surgeon in Orlando, and not just because of his technical skill. We've met former patients who actually named their children after him because of how selflessly he served them in a medical crisis. I will never forget what he said to Priscilla when we first met. She was very apprehensive because her previous surgery had not only failed, it had made her worse. He looked directly at her and said, "Priscilla, you're going to be just fine. You're the kind of patient I love to fix."

Sometimes being the giving one simply means giving confidence and reassurance to those you serve, and Dr. Williamson did exactly that. We walked out of that clinic knowing we were in good hands—and that's a feeling *every* customer wants, not only when a life is at stake.

Priscilla spent sixty-four days in the hospital, followed by several months at home recovering. When she was finally back to good health, despite my joy I was exhausted, depleted, and depressed. I had lived sixty-five years without being depressed for a day, but suddenly it hit me like a ton of bricks. I was lucky to find another giver: Dr. Roderick Hundley, a psychiatrist whose empathy matches his skills. Dr. Hundley not only diagnosed my problem in an hour and prescribed the right treatment and medication, he told me to contact him anytime, 24/7, and gave me his home phone number, his cell number, and his e-mail address. Not only that, he gave me hope, compassion, and the reassurance—which I desperately needed—that everything was going to be okay.

How can you do the equivalent for your customers? How about your employees? Don't forget, if you want them to be the giving ones with customers, you need to be the giving one with them.

I know it's not always easy to follow Tristan's rule and give selflessly, without any thought to ourselves. During Priscilla's long period of recovery, I was her full-time caregiver. For much of that time, she could not get out of bed without assistance. She could not shower, wash her hair, or even go to the bathroom without help. I never left home for more than fifteen minutes because I wanted to be there whenever she needed anything, and she needed a lot. I won't lie: it was hard. I had to be the giving one every day, all the time. Priscilla was not always a good patient, and I was not always a good caregiver. But the truth is, taking care of her was the most satisfying task I've ever taken on. I discovered the truth of what wise people have always said: It *is* better to give than to receive, and to think of others before yourself. As a bonus, Priscilla and I got to know each other better than ever, and we learned that we love each other more than we knew.

Don't take my word for it—or that of philosophers and saints, for that matter. There's solid research on the subject. Some studies have found that people who engage in service work, such as helping the needy, are healthier, feel happier, and live longer. Research also shows that serving others improves mood, increases life satisfaction, lowers stress, and strengthens the immune response. A recent report summarizing a number of major studies found that those who volunteer have greater longevity, less depression, and a lower incidence of heart disease.

I know what you're thinking: What does taking care of an ailing spouse or volunteering at a hospital or a homeless shelter have to do with business? At work,

I'm just doing my job, and I get paid for it. True enough, but you can still choose to do that job in a way that is selfless, by giving your time, energy, and compassion to your customers.

I understand that serving customers can sometimes be downright miserable. They can show up in a lousy mood. They can be self-centered and unreasonable. They can be nasty and abusive. Look at this as an opportunity to give them something, even if it's as trivial as a smile that will boost their mood, a compliment that will inflate their ego, or a helpful hint that will alleviate their frustration. In the end, doing so will have a tremendous upside. Those customers will leave feeling positive about you and your company and will be far more likely to do business with you again. And you'll find that you too are left feeling better about yourself and your company. *You* know you gave of yourself. *You* know you went above and beyond and did your best to serve. That is the best reward of all. That it also pays off on the bottom line is icing on the cake.

I speak to lots of groups and meet a lot of people whose job descriptions involve serving others selflessly, in hospitals, schools, government, and elsewhere. In 2011, for instance, I went to Iraq to give thirteen leadership workshops to U.S. military and State Department personnel, and the following year I spoke to U.S. Navy SEALs at their base in California. I can tell you without a doubt that there are hundreds of thousands of people out there—our military men and women, nurses, teachers, people in nonprofit organizations, and volunteers in all kinds of organizations—who are dedicated to being the giving ones. You can be such a person in your organization, and I assure you it feels really good.

Rule #23

If They Say They Want Horses, Give Them a Motorcar

Henry Ford is alleged to have said, "If I'd asked people what they wanted, they would have said faster horses." His point was that customers do not always know they want or need something until someone invents it—in Ford's case, a motorcar. Many great entrepreneurs and inventors have subscribed to this theory. Steve Jobs, for example, rejected focus groups because he couldn't imagine that consumers would know what products they wanted until Apple showed them.

Once, I stopped in a small shop in Vail, Colorado, to buy a pair of fingernail clippers. As the fellow at the cash register was ringing me up, he asked if I would like a cup of coffee. I didn't know I wanted a cup of coffee until he planted the idea in my head, and the aroma from the freshly brewed pot behind the counter sealed the deal. Turned out I *did* want a cup of coffee after all. I made a point of returning to that shop several times.

Whatever your company offers, whether it's high-end computers or nail clippers, anticipating your customers' needs is one of the best ways to gain a competitive advantage. And in the realm of customer service, anticipation is even more important, because it allows you to solve problems *before* they arise. It also sends a strong signal that you understand your customers and have given serious thought to what will make them happy.

Here's another example of how anticipation can surprise and delight customers. One night I was having dinner at the Four Seasons Resort in Dallas with my business associate Vijay Bajaj, his wife, Reshma, and their ten-year-old son, Armaan. They had just flown in from London and were tired and jet-lagged. Understandably, as dinner progressed, Armaan got sleepier and sleepier. He was just about to plop his head down in his plate of food when out of nowhere our server arrived with a blanket and a pillow. Then, before we could even utter a word, he put two chairs together to make a bed that was just the right length for Armaan to stretch out on. What anticipation! The server saw how tired Armaan was and anticipated that he would need to lie down before his parents finished dinner. And somehow the restaurant had anticipated such moments by keeping blankets and pillows readily available.

One of the best ways to hone your anticipation

skills is to observe (or listen to) customers interacting with your co-workers or employees. See what goes wrong, or *almost* goes wrong, and ask yourself how it might have been prevented. Notice when customers get impatient or sound frustrated. How could that have been avoided, and how could your colleagues have responded better to the upsets?

I recommend that a few times a year you sit down with your team for the sole purpose of brainstorming what products or services your customers might want in the future. Every person on the team should have permission to shout out every idea they can think of, and someone should write them down on a flip chart or a whiteboard. Welcome each idea without judgment, criticism, or evaluation. It might not be practical or prudent to implement all or even most of these ideas right away, and that's fine. But be sure to keep them on file and review that file periodically. A weak or outrageous idea today may turn out to be a powerful innovation a year from now.

Remember, you are never finished anticipating customer needs. Customers have short memories, and their desires are always changing as circumstances, technologies, and public expectations evolve. Often, once a need is met, customers get used to it and replace it with a new one. If you anticipate and honor your customers' need for a motorcar—even when they say they want horses— you can anticipate that they will honor your need to keep their business.

Don't Just Make Promises,
Make Guarantees

D on't make promises you can't keep." Your mom probably told you that when you were a kid, and like most of Mom's advice (see Rule #5, "Ask Yourself, 'What Would Mom Do?'"), it's a good maxim to follow in business as well as in life. No matter what your company offers, no customer should have to work at figuring out what to expect from you. So make your promises explicit, make them crystal clear, and make them known to both your customers *and* your fellow employees. Put them in writing, and post them prominently where everyone can see them, both on your premises and on your website.

Our local Publix supermarket has a three-by-four-foot sign posted to the back wall, where customers can't miss it as they check out. It says:

PUBLIX GUARANTEE
We will never knowingly disappoint you.
If for any reason your purchase does not
give you complete satisfaction,
the full purchase price will be cheerfully refunded
immediately upon request.

There is no way to misunderstand this guarantee. It is unequivocal, and every employee knows how to fulfill it, immediately and cheerfully. A crystal clear guarantee like that one announces that you stand behind your products and services and that you have confidence in your ability to consistently meet your customers' needs. And the current manager of that Publix store, Steve Hungerford, reinforces the message by spending much of his time in the store aisles helping customers and setting a great example for the rest of his team.

Now here's an example of a promise that needs some work. It's from Pearle Vision.

We want you to be happy with your new glasses.
That's why we'll repair or exchange them for up to
30 days at no charge to you. This guarantee does
not cover accidental damage, scratches, or breakage.
Valid at participating locations.

Note that last sentence. It means that any of the Pearle franchises can choose not to honor that guarantee.

If it were up to me, the phrase *Valid at participating locations* would be struck from the English language. I don't understand why a franchise operation would not insist that every single store have the same guarantee. The next-to-last sentence doesn't exactly make you feel warm and fuzzy, either. Maybe it's necessary to prevent people from requesting a full refund when they step on their own glasses or run over them in the driveway. But wouldn't it be better to state what you *do* guarantee instead of what you don't? A well-stated guarantee not only reassures your customers, it is also a form of branding because it states publicly what your company stands for—and what it will *not* stand for.

An excellent service guarantee should not only be plainly visible and easy to understand, it should also do the following:

* Include explicit details. "Your new tires will be installed in 60 minutes" is a lot stronger than "We will install your tires as quickly as possible." Even stronger is "If your tires are not installed in 60 minutes, we'll do it for free." That kind of clarity tells the customer exactly what to expect and eliminates arguments based on misunderstanding.

* Tell customers exactly *how* to reach you to make good on the guarantee. On a website? What's the URL? By e-mail? What's the address? Telephone? What number do they call?

Written letter? To what postal address? In person? Where?

* Minimize exceptions. A guarantee should be *unconditional*, like the one at Publix. Guarantees with a long list of exceptions are hardly worth the paper they're printed on.

* Be meaningful to your customers. If your average customer is generally in a hurry, a guarantee for fast service will matter to them. If your average customer cares most about luxury or about convenience, you should tailor your guarantee accordingly.

* Clearly state the reward if the guarantee is not met. If customers are not happy, do they get a cash refund? A credit? A free product or service the next time they do business with you?

* Make the reward easy to redeem. Don't put your customers through a bureaucratic maze or force them to fill out endless forms or speak to a dozen strangers on the phone.

The bottom line is that customers want to know that you care, and a good guarantee sends that message. But the best guarantee in the world will backfire on you if you treat it only as a marketing gimmick and follow through on its promises grudgingly. In an excellent *Harvard Business Review* article titled "The Power of Unconditional Service Guarantees," Christopher W. L. Hart wrote: "If your aim is to minimize the guarantee's impact on your organization but to maximize its marketing punch, you won't succeed." That was written in 1988, and it's just as true today.

A German proverb says that "promises are like the full moon; if they are not kept at once, they diminish day by day." So please, remember Mom's advice: Don't make a promise you can't keep or don't intend to keep.

Rule #25

Treat Every Customer Like a Regular

Whenever Priscilla and I walk into our favorite restaurant in Orlando, Le Coq au Vin, Sandy, the co-owner, greets us with a hug and says she's happy to see us. We have no doubt that she means it. If we're with friends, we introduce them, and Sandy seems just as happy to see them, too. She escorts us to our favorite table. At some point, her husband, Reimund, who happens also to be the chef, comes by to say hello and tell us if he's cooked up anything special that night. Sometimes he'll send over a bottle of wine—the kind he knows we like. The food is superb, but that alone wouldn't be enough reason to go back again and again. It's the special treatment.

Certainly one aspect of delivering excellent service is to find ways to enhance the experience of repeat customers every time you see them, as Le Coq au Vin does for Priscilla and me. But there's another point to be made: Even a first-time guest can be treated like a VIP customer. In fact, the reason Priscilla and I became frequent guests of this restaurant in the first place was that we were treated as special right from the beginning. I can remember how surprised I was the first time the owners called us by name, remembered where we asked to be seated on our previous visit, and saved that table for us when I made my reservation.

Don't think this applies only to high-end restaurants. Someone recently told me a story about a visit to his neighborhood coffee shop. The group ahead of him on line was taking a lot of time making up their minds about their order. My friend started to get impatient. Then he spotted a woman behind the counter waving him over. When he got there, she handed him his usual drink—a large decaf cappuccino. He was astonished. He didn't think anyone would remember his face, let alone his usual order. He told me he'll be going to that coffee shop a lot more often now. We all like to be treated as though we're special, and great businesses fulfill that need for every customer who walks through their doors. Not long ago, I walked in cold to a Verizon Wireless retail store. I'd been dissatisfied with my cell phone provider and thought I'd check out an alternative. The woman who took care of me, Angela Pak, was so upbeat, knowledgeable, and totally focused that I still remember her name. She steered me to just the right device, and she gave me all the time I needed to make up my mind. Largely because of Angela's attentive service, I switched carriers, even though it was going to cost me a couple of hundred bucks to get out of my previous contract. The key was that she homed in on what I needed from a phone and quickly found a way to satisfy that need.

You'd be surprised how easy it is to learn something unique about a customer and use the knowledge to make that person feel special. The clue might come from something a man is wearing, or a woman's accent, or someone's body language and tone of voice, or the magazine a person is carrying, or a snatch of conversation that tells you a couple is in that city for the first time or that one of them is really in the mood for dessert or a glass of champagne. Close observation can also reveal a customer's underlying mood. Is he or she impatient or in a hurry? If so, make an extra effort to serve him or her more quickly. Worried? Take the extra time to address his or her concerns. Depressed? Maybe offer a compliment or tell a light joke to boost his or her mood. Those moods may have nothing to do with you or the interaction the customer is having with your company, but if you are tuned in to them, they can reveal how that individual customer wants to be treated.

In short, do whatever you can to make regular customers feel like family and new customers feel like regulars. Remember the theme song from the TV series *Cheers*? Don't you want to go "where everybody knows your name, and they're always glad you came"? Make all your customers feel that you're really glad they came. Because no matter what anyone says, when it comes to service, familiarity does *not* breed contempt, it breeds repeat business.

Rule #26

Serve to WIN

That's not a sports metaphor. WIN is an acronym for "what's important now." And what's important now is what you have to focus on if you want your customers to feel well served. Their needs, their desires, their concerns—that's what's important now. Not cleaning up the vacated table, or folding the shirts that were left in the dressing room, or finishing up that phone call while the client or customer is waiting. Not gossiping with co-workers. Not watching the talking baby or the dancing panda on YouTube. I've seen employees do all of the above and more. They're all signs of a business that lacks a customer service ethic or that talks the talk but does not walk it.

I can tell you from long personal experience as both a manager and a consumer, there's no bigger turnoff to a customer than being ignored, even for a few seconds, especially for a non-work-related reason. That's why you should be paying attention to your customers at all times. Obviously, if you work in a retail store, a restaurant, a bank, or any business with direct contact with customers or clients, there are times when you're very busy and people have to wait to get your complete attention. Customers will inevitably enter while you're serving someone else. WIN still applies. What's important now? Obviously, the customer you're currently serving is your highest priority. But you can *also* let the new customers know they've been seen. A nod, a gesture, some brief eye contact, a pleasant "I'll be right with you. Please make yourself comfortable"—that's all it takes. People want to be acknowledged. Ignore them and they'll either leave or get so annoyed and sullen that they'll be impossible to please when you finally pay attention to them.

You may think you're doing what you're supposed to be doing by cleaning up that vacated table or folding those shirts in the dressing room. You may even be following procedure. But there is more to what's important now than completing a task that has to be done or executing the transaction your job description calls for. There's also a vital emotional aspect to service. As business consultant and author Stephen Denning put it, "It's not about a transaction; it's about forging a relationship." At an airport recently, I was one of about 150 passengers waiting at the gate as takeoff time approached, wondering why we hadn't started boarding yet. As we milled about, anxiously imagining what might be going on and hoping to get an explanation, the attendant behind the desk kept talking on the phone, doing her best to look away from us. She was obviously doing her job by speaking on the phone, but she wasn't doing a good one in terms of WIN. That phone call was important. But so were the nervous passengers. If she'd simply paused and made a brief announcement, or even just held up her hand and looked a few of us in the eye, things would have calmed down. Instead, the minute she hung up, she was besieged by angry passengers, some of whom will never fly that airline again if they can help it.

What's important now is not always immediately obvious. It requires judgment and sensitivity, and some people are born with those qualities. If you're a manager, these are the people you want to hire. But even if not everyone on your team was born with a WIN intuition, you can still make sure everyone knows that what's most important in every *now* is satisfying the customers' emotional needs. Everything else can wait.

Rule #27

Make ASAP Your Standard Deadline

We live in an era of instant gratification. People want what they want, and they want it now. ASAP has become our standard deadline as a society, and when it comes to serving customers, it should be your deadline as well.

The old saying "Speed kills" may be true for drugs and driving, but it's the opposite in business. In our impatient, fast-paced world, if you can develop a reputation for getting things done faster than your competitors, you will have a huge advantage.

Not long ago, I got home from a business trip on a Saturday evening and turned on my computer. Instead of the usual desktop screen, I was greeted by a scary error message that may as well have been written in a foreign language. I decided to go to bed and try again in the morning, hoping that time heals computers as it does other wounds. On Sunday morning, I tried again.

Same gobbledygook message. I needed help badly, because I had to work on something that was archived only on that computer.

So I used my smartphone to search for repair services in my area that might be open on a Sunday morning. Google rolled out a long list of websites, each one promising computer repair miracles. I phoned the first two and got messages telling me to leave my number and they would call me back. They didn't say when. The next two said they worked Monday through Friday and wished me a good weekend, without even the option to leave a message. I was not having a good weekend. A couple of hours later, having received no callbacks, I returned to Google, where I spotted an ad that offered service 24/7. I called the number, and to my astonishment a human being answered the phone. His name was Graham. I described my problem as best I could, and Graham told me to bring my computer over to his home. When I got there, he said he could probably fix it within twenty-four hours.

At four p.m. *that day*, Graham called. "Your computer is ready," he said. "It's working just fine now." That's when I realized how good early feels when it really matters.

Graham is not only technically skilled, he's a smart businessman. He's made ASAP his deadline, and he knows that it's far better to underpromise and overdeliver than vice versa. This strategy can be applied to virtually any business. Work in retail? If you think the back-ordered item will arrive on Wednesday, tell the customer Thursday, then call to say it came in early. Run an auto shop? Tell the customer her car will be ready at five p.m. and call her at two to say you got it done for her early. Work in finance, insurance, or banking? Set the voice mail system on your phone line to say the hold time is five minutes, then pick up in two. As I learned from this computer repair experience, few things feel better than the pleasant surprise of being served faster than you expected to be.

Today, ASAP is more highly valued than ever. So sit down with your team ASAP and think up new systems and processes for getting the job done faster, sooner, earlier. That should be your motto, just as "Faster, higher, stronger" is to Olympic athletes. Trust me, when it comes to service, speed matters.

Rule #28

Know the Difference
Between Needs and Wants

Customers come to you for something they need, or think they need, whether it's a shirt, a meal, a smartphone, roof repair, a checking account, or a luxury vacation. This is what gets them in the door. But if you want to keep them coming back and singing your praises, it's not enough to give them what they need; you have to also give them what they *really want*.

Your customers may all have more or less the same apparent need, but that doesn't mean they all want the same thing. Everyone needs certain basics, like food, leisure, clothing, transportation, health care, and so on. Different *wants* are what give us both burger chains and Whole Foods, vintage clothing stores and Neiman Marcus, campsites and luxury cruises, SUVs and hybrids.

Customers' wants can be just as varied when it comes to service. Some customers just want to be served quickly and efficiently. Others care most about convenience. Still others just want the best possible deal. And for some, the quality of human interaction ranks highest; they want to be treated with warmth, friendliness, and respect. Being able to ferret out and deliver what each customer wants *most* will go a long way toward winning you their repeat business and their loyalty.

I sometimes shop at Walmart, but it's not for their "everyday low prices." I go because the store is close to my house, is open twenty-four hours a day, and has very fast checkout. Shopping there saves me time, and saving time is what I happen to want. I would pay everyday *high* prices if it meant I could get in and out of there quickly.

Here's another way to look at it: Products and services are needs; wants are about the experience of obtaining them. Needs are obvious and practical; wants are subtle and usually emotional. Health insurance is a need; wants include low premiums, expert advice, and speedy resolution of claims. Car repair is a need; wants include honesty, a clear explanation of the problem, and quick, reliable completion of the work. A cup of coffee is a need; wants include good taste and fast, pleasant service. A cell phone provider is a need; wants are reliable reception, expert tech support, and a hassle-free process for redeeming upgrades.

One woman shared a story with me that illustrates the power of discerning a customer's wants. She had been working at hospices for ten years when she suddenly lost her job. She was worn out and money was tight, but she needed to have her hair cut, so she went to a salon. The hairdresser, she said, "washed my hair with such care that I was certain I was being attended by the fingers of God. Someone who knew nothing about me was giving me service with the same comforting energy and spirit that I gave to the dying and their families for a decade. I *needed* a hair trim, but what I really *wanted* was some comfort and care. This young woman sensed that. I will never forget her. This is the only place I go now to get my hair done." That hairdresser knew the difference between a need and a want.

Figuring out exactly what your customers want sounds like a no-brainer, but it is not always easy. When I was at Disney, we always thought we knew what our guests wanted when they came to our theme parks and hotels: good shows, exciting rides, and fun. Then we engaged the Gallup organization to survey six thousand recent guests and ask them one question: "What do you expect when you come to Walt Disney World?" Turned out they wanted what we thought they did, but they took those things for granted. They were more like needs. Their top four *wants*, on the other hand, were these:

* Make us feel special.
* Treat us as individuals.
* Show respect to us.
* Be knowledgeable.

That experience taught me that customers' wants often run deep. It also taught me that the only way to make sure you meet their wants and not just their needs is to delve beneath the surface and probe their deeper perceptions and emotions. You can learn about the wants of your customer base as a whole through formal surveys like the one I just mentioned and also by informally asking people—not just your actual customers, but friends, neighbors, and complete strangers—what they really want when they do business with a company like yours.

Figuring out what individual customers want is a bigger challenge, because each person prioritizes his or her wants differently. So if you're dealing with customers directly, you should try to get a window on their unique personalities. To this end, I can't overemphasize the value—and the power—of focused listening (see Rule #17, "Listen Up"). When people speak, clues to their moods and emotions are usually expressed in their choice of words, their tone of voice, even their faces and gestures. What prompts them to sound skeptical? When does their voice show signs of enthusiasm? When do they seem to lose interest? Do they sound impatient? These signs can be subtle and hard to interpret, which is why it's crucial that you pay close attention. A puzzled look, for example, can mean they need more details or a simpler explanation. A blank stare can mean "I have no clue what you are talking about, but I would like to learn more" or "Is she wasting my time with this?"

What a customer doesn't say can also speak volumes. When customers go from being talkative and inquisitive to silent and withdrawn, it's usually a sign that you're losing their interest and you'd better dig deeper to find out what they want.

You should also be alert to subtle signs in customers' body language. When do they frown? When do their eyes light up? Are they fidgeting? Are they folding their arms in a defensive posture? That can mean "I don't like what I am hearing" or "I'm not going to let this person put one over on me." Sometimes you can also find clues in their personal appearance; someone who is dressed impeccably in expensive clothes, for instance, might value quality and self-image over low prices, whereas someone in a comfortable old outfit might want durability more than the fashionable new style. Those examples may help you spot clues about a customer's wants, but in truth there are few hard-and-fast rules. Experience is the best teacher when it comes to reading other human beings.

Here is an example of how focused listening can clue you in to customers' wants. A woman called tech support with a computer problem. The phone rep guided her through some simple steps to diagnose the problem, but the caller kept getting flustered and had to start over several times. Instead of losing patience, the rep listened carefully. He noticed that the woman's voice was cracking and she sounded not just confused but distraught. Gently and patiently, he asked if she was okay. Then she poured out her heart. She had recently lost her college-age son in an accident. Dealing with the software problem in the aftermath of such a tragedy was especially hard because her son used to take care of all her computer needs. She needed to have the glitch solved, but her really deep *want* was to express her sorrow. The support person understood that and let her speak at length about her son. Not surprisingly, his company earned her loyalty—and added revenue for the extended service contract that also ended up being a source of comfort and security for the grieving mother.

Bottom line: Your products may be so good that the world will beat a path to your door. But that path goes two ways, and it will lead straight to the doors of your competitors if you stop at giving customers only what they need. Dig deeper and give them what they *want*, even if they don't know they want it.

Rule #29

Have a Geek on Your Team

There were always good reasons for businesses to hire young people: They look good; they have strong bodies; they work for low wages; and the competent ones move on to excel in higher roles in the company. Nowadays, there's another reason: They're way more likely than their older counterparts to be tuned in to the latest technologies, and some of them are real experts. I recently heard someone say, "The geek shall inherit the earth." I wouldn't go that far, but I will say that if your company doesn't have a few technology geeks in its ranks, you're at a competitive disadvantage. It seems that every day brings some new electronic innovation that can improve customer service, so you'd better have people on board who are plugged into the high-tech world, preferably with the know-how to do some innovating themselves.

Recently, I read that the sixty-thousand-square-foot Orchard Supply Hardware store in San José, California, instituted something called "zoned service." What in the world is zoned service? Mark Baker, the CEO of the company, whose store is a member of Do It Best Corp., a cooperative of four thousand stores worldwide, explained it this way: "Everybody is wearing a headset in the store, so we can deploy our resources to where the customers need help, whether it's loading in the parking lot or more information on products." That's a good example of management using technology to better serve customers. It's also proof that there is always a way to do things better, and these days the chances are good that it will be a geek who comes up with it.

The dictionary defines "geek" as

* an enthusiast or expert, especially in a technological field or activity;
* a person with an eccentric devotion to a particular interest;
* a person who is interested in technology, especially computing and new media.

Companies need these kinds of people, today more than ever, because now, regardless of the business you're in, technology invariably affects the quality of service you can offer your customers. Technology can help streamline your sales procedures. It can make it easier for customers to find and buy your products online. It can help you better identify your target customers and get their attention. And, of course, it can make it easier for customers to ask questions, make suggestions, express complaints, return goods, and get their problems taken care of expeditiously. You *need* technology if you want to stay alive in today's competitive environment. Think about it this way: If your competitor's technological upgrade saves customers just a few minutes of their precious time, or prevents just one hassle, or makes their interaction with the company a bit more pleasant, you have lost.

Even if your version of being "high-tech" is hosting a website and a Facebook page, or maintaining a computerized database, you need a geek squad to make sure all the systems are up-to-date and operating at maximum efficiency. At a time when technology is advancing at a faster and faster clip, you need geeks not only to set up your systems and keep them humming, but also to keep up with ever-changing trends. As national security expert Richard Clarke once said, "Geeks get it done."

Bear in mind that your ideal geek is not just an expert in technology, but also a caring individual who understands the value of customer service. A techie with empathy is what you're after, someone who can imagine walking in the shoes of your customers and see the ways technology can be used to give them exactly what they want.

Our world has been transformed by geeks. Your business can be, too. So bring some into your company or onto your team, and give them the salaries, the respect, and the creative space they need to elevate your service to new heights.

Rule #30

Be Relentless About Details

Richard Branson, the British entrepreneur who founded the Virgin Group, once wrote that "the only difference between merely satisfactory delivery and great delivery is attention to detail." That's doubly true for delivering great customer service.

Few companies are as attentive to detail as the shipping giant FedEx. Despite having more than three hundred thousand employees in 220 countries and territories worldwide, FedEx provides each and every one of its drivers with daily driving directions that are carefully calibrated to include the shortest distance between all points and as many right turns as possible, in order to speed up delivery times and conserve fuel. Think of the time and money such attention to detail saves in an operation as big as FedEx, and think about how it enables them to provide faster and less expensive deliveries for their customers.

When you first opened your business or started in your present position, you probably paid great attention to detail, keeping everything spotless and running like a well-oiled machine. Is it still that way? If not, you're not alone; it's common for attention to detail to deteriorate over time. Details have enemies, and they include time, success, and experience. It's only human nature to start ignoring the little stuff when you're busy or when things are going well. As tasks become routine and we take our own expertise for granted, we become so familiar with the forest that we stop seeing the trees.

But while getting a bit careless is natural, it can also have dire consequences. Think about the tragedies that can occur when doctors or nurses, truck drivers or auto mechanics, firefighters or security personnel, and so on lose sight of details like one loose screw on a wheel, one broken turn signal, or one misplaced digit on a prescription. True, in most jobs and businesses, neglecting details will not cost you lives, but it will cost you customers and, in turn, profits.

One deceptively simple but incredibly effective tool for keeping yourself and others focused on details is the checklist. Atul Gawande, a surgeon, Harvard Medical School professor, and author, writes in his bestselling book, *The Checklist Manifesto*, that checklists can be used to prevent mishaps ranging from minor annoyances to fatal errors in every imaginable setting. In hospitals, for instance, data show that using checklists to ensure cleanliness can dramatically reduce infections. In aviation, checklists improve operational efficiencies and decrease the number of crashes. In fact, Gawande presents compelling evidence that checklists can reduce human errors in everything from construction to investment banking to homeland security. If checklists can help hospitals enhance patient safety, or construction sites prevent worker injuries, they can certainly help you and your organization ensure customer satisfaction.

Naturally, checklists will vary depending on the business, the department, the employee's function, and the conditions at the time. Here's what a customer service checklist might look like for a typical retail business:

- ☐ Driveway, parking lot, and front entrance are spotless and inviting.
- ☐ All team members look professional and are dressed appropriately.
- ☐ Name tags are on straight and clearly visible.
- ☐ Lighting and music are at the proper level.
- ☐ All merchandise is displayed perfectly.
- ☐ Special sale items are clearly displayed.
- ☐ Checkout area is free of clutter and checkout personnel are in place.
- ☐ Restrooms are spotless and smell fresh and clean.
- ☐ Magazines in the waiting area are current and stacked neatly.
- ☐ Fresh coffee has been brewed and is ready to be offered to customers.

☐ Employees are ready to greet customers upon arrival.

☐ Employee entrance, break room, and locker room are clean and inviting.

☐ All elevators are clean and operational.

☐ Computers are booted up and working.

☐ Printers have enough paper.

Here are a few other best practices of detail-oriented businesses that you can implement to improve service in your organization:

* Develop specific, detailed policies and procedures, and communicate them clearly to everyone who interacts directly or indirectly with customers.

* Allow frequent breaks to make sure employees in routine, repetitive jobs stay alert.

* Regularly inspect machinery, equipment, and technology to make sure everything is running smoothly.

* Create an early warning system by training *all* your employees to spot potential problems and giving them safe, easy ways to report them.

* Build a culture of open communication, so employees at every level can easily connect with those who are empowered to take action.

* Walk your operation every day with a pad or a clipboard. Make note of every detail that is not

quite right and immediately set about making corrections. Your employees or colleagues may think you're obsessive at first, but they'll quickly learn to respect your attention to detail—and to emulate it.

They say that the devil is in the details. Well, in business that's true only if you neglect them. If you pay attention to those devilish details, it will pay off in better service, higher profits, and lasting customer appreciation.

Rule #31

Be Reliable

Businesses live or die based on their reliability. You can have the best product in the world, but it won't be enough to keep you profitable if you don't reliably give your customers what they expect, when they expect it, each and every time. No matter what your business is, being reliable makes your customers feel safe and secure. They want to know that their package will be delivered on time just as much as they want to know that their car will start when they turn the key, or that the pizza will be hot when it gets to their house, or that their hotel room will be clean when they check in.

Reliability lies at the heart of your company's reputation and, in turn, your profitability. Charles Fombrun, a professor of management at New York University's Stern School of Business, has written that "a reputation develops from a company's uniqueness and from identity-shaping practices, maintained over time, that lead stakeholders to perceive the company as credible, reliable, responsible and trustworthy." He added this: "By increasing our faith and confidence in the company's actions, credibility and reliability create economic value." Fombrun cited a study that identified reliability as one of the top ten factors that determine a corporation's reputation and included "provides consistent service" in its definition of reliability.

If that doesn't convince you, think of it this way. Suppose your local dry cleaner does a great job of cleaning and pressing clothes and removing stains. They charge low prices and always greet you by name and with a smile. But about 10 percent of the time your shirts aren't ready when promised. Wouldn't that be enough to make you look for another cleaner? Or suppose the restaurant that serves up your favorite tuna melt with friendly service and good prices is occasionally so slow in bringing your food that you're late getting back to the office? How long before you're eating someplace else? Suppose you have an auto mechanic who diagnoses problems like Sherlock Holmes, does impeccable repair work, and charges reasonable prices but sometimes leaves dirt on the seats and grease on the carpet. Who ya gonna call the next time you need repairs?

As many have observed, it takes a long time to build a good reputation and an instant to lose it. Remember when Toyota recalled 2.3 million cars because of an "unintended acceleration" problem? Overnight, a brand that had been synonymous with safety and dependability was seen as shoddy, or as one newspaper headline put it: TOYOTA RECALL TANKS RELIABILITY AND REPUTATION. It took a lot of work, but Toyota regained its well-deserved reputation for reliability and once again enjoys the loyalty of millions of drivers, like Priscilla and me. But most companies find it very hard to bounce back when they're labeled unreliable, and some never do. When a business, product, or service that had been considered reliable betrays our trust, it jolts our senses. That's when we start asking our friends questions like "Where do you get your shirts cleaned?" and "Do you have a reliable mechanic?"

If you want to keep your loyal customers, you need to maintain a stellar reputation for reliable service in both routine circumstances and exceptional situations. You don't want people saying of your company, "They do great work most of the time, but I can't count on them." To a business, that's a death sentence. You may not notice your customers' absence until it shows up on your quarterly report. But by then, it will probably be too late to get those customers back. If, on the other hand, your company is synonymous with reliable service, customers will pay more and travel farther to do business with you instead of with a less reliable competitor.

And no matter how big your company is, its reputation depends on the reliability of every single employee. That's why early chapters in this book emphasize the importance of hiring the right people, training them well, updating and upgrading their skills, and testing them along the way to make sure the training takes hold. Of course, as Rule #38 ("Keep Doing It Better") makes plain, being consistent does not mean that you and your employees shouldn't make changes that improve your service. What matters is not that the procedures themselves are exactly the same at all times, it's that the *quality of service* is consistently great.

There should never be any exceptions to that.

Rule #32

Don't Give the Responsibility
Without the Authority

A couple I know recently went to a large electronics store to buy a hot new gaming system that was just about to be released. They arrived before the store opened and lined up with other game aficionados. Because the wife had health problems and was in a wheelchair, they asked a security guard if they could wait inside the mall instead of outdoors in the sun. The guard went inside to check. Twenty minutes later, she returned and told the couple they would have to wait outside with everyone else. They asked to speak to a manager. Impossible, they were told. There was nothing a manager could do. Rules were rules. End of story.

Common sense would suggest that the guard should have been able to make an exception for a handicapped customer. But clearly this guard had not been given the authority to make an autonomous judgment, even for something this obvious. The result was an extremely irritated customer and a lost sale of a high-margin item.

One company that knows how to empower its employees to make decisions is Amazon. I remember when Priscilla called customer service because she had a problem with a set of china she had ordered. Instead of putting her on hold while he checked with a supervisor or manager, the phone rep immediately offered to credit Priscilla's card or send her a replacement. Priscilla was so impressed that she told the agent her husband was writing a book on customer service and would be interested to know more about the company's policies. "It's simple," the agent said. "We have the authority to make our customers happy."

Every employee who deals with customers should know that their number one responsibility is to make those customers happy, and they should be given the authority they need to ensure that outcome. Of course, there are always limits to that authority, but those limits have to be accompanied by solid procedures that guarantee that the person who *does* have authority is always accessible. As you probably know from your own experience, it's agonizing to be told you have to speak to a supervisor and then be kept waiting forever.

Research clearly shows that it is not the problem itself that drives customers away, it's how poorly you resolve the problem and how slowly you resolve it. These days, consumers want what they want, and they want it now, hassle-free. With every minute they have to wait to get an issue resolved, and with every irritation they have to endure along the way, the odds increase that they'll find another place to do business next time. Plus, the more authority frontline employees have, the fewer times managers will have to be called away from their other duties.

One reason Disney World has a worldwide reputation for excellent service is that the company keeps careful records of all problems and mishaps that occur at the park, then trains and authorizes employees to take care of those problems right on the spot. I strongly suggest that you do the equivalent in your area of responsibility: survey both employees and customers on a regular basis, so you know where problems typically arise. Then equip all employees with the training they need to handle any issue that might crop up, and give them the authority to take action.

A friend of mine once told me about the time he arrived at an airport only to discover that he had accidentally made his reservation for the wrong day. When he learned that his flight had left twenty-four hours earlier, his heart dropped into his shoes. He was flying to a business meeting, and if he couldn't get on another flight, he was in big trouble. "Let me see what I can do," said the ticket agent. As my friend sweated it out, the agent simply tapped a bunch of computer keys. A few short minutes later, she said, "You're all set. Your flight leaves in forty minutes." He thanked her profusely and whipped out his credit card to pay the penalty for changing flights. She waved it away. No charge.

Obviously, this agent had been given the authority by her company, Southwest Airlines, to do whatever she could to help a customer. Organizations that adopt a similar policy will be rewarded with loyal customers and a nice bottom line.

Rule #33

Never, Ever Argue with a Customer

When I was running the restaurant at a Marriott Hotel back in 1976, there was a regular diner who would complain to me every time she came in. Her tea was too cold. Her soup was too hot. Why didn't we serve X? Why *did* we serve Y? The entrée came too quickly. The wine didn't come quickly enough. At one point, I couldn't take it anymore and my inner wise guy got the better of me. "Do you lie awake at night thinking up things to complain about when you come in here?" I asked her.

She promptly snapped back. Before I knew it, we were arguing. I told her the tea was quite hot; she insisted it was cold. I said the soup was just the right temperature; she contended that it burned her tongue. Pretty soon the argument got personal. It was no longer about tea and soup; it was about winning and losing. Later, Bud Davis, the general manager, called me into his office and chewed me out. I not only had to apologize to that woman, I had to practically kiss her feet every day from then on. I did as instructed, but inside I was furious, because I felt that she'd won. Then Bud taught me an important lesson: When the customer wins, it's really the company that has won.

Think about it this way, he told me: Even the most obnoxious customers want to give you their business, and their money is worth exactly the same amount as that of the sweet, kind, gracious customers. So if I wanted to keep taking those customers' money, I would be well-advised to keep my mouth shut. Lesson learned. I never argued with a customer again. And once I became an executive, I always made sure that no one on my teams ever did so, either. Of course, I had to bite my tongue more than once in my career. But my tongue survived, and the companies I worked for were spared the loss of quite a few customers. As my grandson Jullian reminded me recently, the human tongue is the strongest muscle in the body. When a customer picks an argument, you'd be wise to refrain from flexing that muscle.

From time to time over the years, a customer would complain to me that a frontline employee had been belligerent. When I asked the employee what happened, I'd usually be told that the customer was wrong about the facts, or had been abusive, or was trying to cheat the company. Most of the time, the employee believed it was better to lose a bad customer than appease one. They were surprised when I told them there's no such thing as a "bad" customer.

I always made sure those employees learned what Bud Davis taught me: Never, ever argue with a customer. Don't get defensive. Don't get rude. Don't get sarcastic. Period. Will some customers try to scam you? Sure. Will some try to take advantage of you and get something for free? No doubt. Do some people have a lousy attitude and an outsize sense of entitlement? Oh, yeah. You bet. But none of that matters, because business is business and profit is profit.

So the louder they get, the quieter you should get. The more agitated they become, the calmer you should become. As the old saying goes, "When you argue with an idiot, there are two idiots." If you can't handle a particular situation without losing your cool, walk away and get your manager immediately.

If you are the manager, make sure that your employees know to always be respectful, calm, and in control when dealing with customers, no matter how hard any particular person pushes their buttons. The only emotions they should display to an angry customer are empathy and compassion. The only weapons they should wield are kindness, patience, and competence. Two old maxims apply: (1) The customer is always right; and (2) Grin and bear it. Bear it while the customer vents, then fix whatever triggered the customer's rage.

When a customer has a tantrum, it is vital not to take it personally. The anger is not about you—the customer doesn't even know you or care about you—it is about a situation. He's been disappointed or frustrated. Maybe she feels ripped off. The complaint may be totally unreasonable, and the reaction may be way over the top. Or not. Either way, it's not about *you*. It's about the circumstances. You're just the available outlet for the customer's rage. Fix whatever is wrong and you become the hero rather than the target.

Keep this in mind, too: Everyone has problems that you don't know about. The customer screaming at you may have had the worst day of her life, and what happened at your business was the final straw. Maybe she lost her job. Maybe a loved one died. Maybe she just got a horrible medical diagnosis. Why make her day worse than it already is by drawing her into an argument?

One New Year's Eve decades ago, at the same Marriott Hotel where Bud Davis read me the riot act, an angry customer demanded to see the manager. That manager was me. The customer was irate because when he and his wife had arrived at the restaurant to ring in the new year, he had been told that there was no record of their reservation. We were completely sold out, and the place was packed. I told him that the hostess was right: every table was booked. His fury escalated to blind rage. He shouted in the crudest of terms that I was an idiot and my employees were losers. I took a deep breath and calmly said I would fix my problem. That's right; I said *my* problem, because it was in fact my problem, not his. But he didn't quite hear me because he was too busy yelling. So I asked firmly but not argumentatively, "Do you want to keep yelling at me, or do you want to let me resolve this issue?" He muttered, "Fix it." And when I said I would, just like that, he calmed down.

I escorted the couple to the bar and ordered champagne for them, on the house. I even gave them two of those pointy New Year's Eve hats (it's hard to throw a tantrum in a funny hat). Then I went to the hotel's banquet department, found a small cocktail table that would seat two, and squeezed it into a corner of the restaurant. Fifteen minutes later, they were seated at the table with a fresh rose and a candle. And a few hours later when he paid his check, the restaurant had made that many more dollars and secured one more happy customer.

Doesn't that sound like a far better alternative to telling a belligerent customer to leave? In addition to the obvious gains, there was another benefit: I set a good example for all the other employees. Don't forget that part of a manager's responsibility is to model right behavior; if you can't check your emotions when you deal with customers—or your staff—then you can't expect anyone else to, either.

Here are some more tips I've picked up over the years for dealing with angry customers without returning fire:

* Let them vent. Listen to the whole story without interrupting. Sometimes all they want is to be heard.

* Take responsibility for the problem. Don't blame. Don't explain. Don't make excuses. Customers don't really care that you were understaffed, or that the delivery van had an accident, or that your Internet server was down.

* Try to come up with a quick, easy solution. If you can't, ask if you can work on the problem and get back to them in twenty-four or forty-eight hours. In my experience, most angry customers calm down after being treated decently and are more likely to accept a reasonable solution later on than they are in the heat of battle.

* Eat humble pie. Even though you should treat the customer as though he is always right, sometimes customers are simply wrong: maybe he misread the agreement form, or wrote down an incorrect date, or doesn't know the facts. In these cases it would be easy to win the argument, but at what cost? Sometimes it's better to let it go. Humble pie can taste pretty good when you get to keep a customer instead of losing her forever.

* Make it easy to complain. Have a hotline, a service desk, or an e-mail account manned by real people who are trained to resolve complaints. Think of it as preventive medicine: an ounce of

complaint today is worth a pound of argument tomorrow.

★ Remember the final score. When you win an argument with a customer, in reality you've *both* lost.

Rule #34

Never Say No—Except "No Problem"

A business traveler I know arrived at the gate about an hour ahead of his 3:40 flight, just in time to spot his boss boarding an earlier flight to the same destination. He asked the gate attendant if the plane was full. "It's about halfway full," was the reply.

"Great," said the traveler. "Can I get on this flight on standby?"

"No."

My acquaintance tried to appeal to common sense. No dice. The answer was no, and that was that.

No one likes hearing the word *no*. It triggers all kinds of negative emotions and reactions. In fact, research indicates that it's not even a good word for parents to use with young children. That's because "no" makes a forbidden activity more intriguing and can even make a child more determined to do it. Well, your grown-up customers are not that different. When they hear "no," their brains shift into defensive mode, making them more determined to change your mind and get you to "yes."

"No" is a hope destroyer. It also signifies a lack of effort. If your first response is a flat-out "no," you're essentially saying that you've taken the easy way out and will not be making any effort to find ways to make the customer happy. That's basically what that airline told me over and over again in that story I shared in Rule #2 ("You Win Customers One at a Time and Lose Them a Thousand at a Time"). My grandson Jullian, who watched the whole situation unfold, said that the difference between that airline and Southwest is that "Southwest says yes."

Remember Nancy Reagan's "Just say no" campaign back in the 1980s? Well, it didn't win the war on drugs, and it surely won't win the war for customer loyalty. For that, you want the exact opposite: Just don't say no! Better yet, add a key word, so it becomes "No problem." As in "No problem. I understand your situation. Let me see what I can do," or "No problem. I'll need to speak to my supervisor. May I call you back in an hour?"

Even in cases where you're unable to grant the customer's request, you should still avoid the word *no*. Phrase your answer in a way that leaves the door open and gives the customer hope: "Let me see what I can do. Can I get back to you on that tomorrow?" Then get to work quickly and find a way to satisfy the request or come up with a reasonable alternative—and make sure you actually *do* follow up when you say you will, if not sooner. The answer may still be no, but don't let that word reach your tongue. Instead, focus on—and lead with—what you *can* do for the customer. Say something like "I can give you a store credit, but I'm sorry to say that I can't refund your money," or "We'll be happy to repair it, but I was not able to get approval to give you a new one." Your customer might be disappointed, but she'll appreciate the sincerity of your effort and will likely keep doing business with you.

In short, saying "no" should be the very last resort. Don't say it until you have exhausted every reasonable way to satisfy the customer, and if it comes down to a flat-out "no," the person who says it should be a manager, a supervisor, or the owner of the business.

What if the customer's request is so outrageous that you not only want to say "no," you want to tell him he's off his rocker? Fight the urge (remember Rule #33, "Never, Ever Argue with a Customer"). Pause, smile, and ask for some time to carefully review the issue— even if you know there's not a snowball's chance in hell that you can give him what he wants. Tell him exactly when you'll get back to him, and follow through on that promise. Most people are far more reasonable after a cooling-down period, especially if they see you've at least put forth an effort.

When I worked at Disney, a young man phoned my office one day, howling mad. He was upset because at a performance in one of the theme parks, a cast member had told his girlfriend to stop taking photos. I explained the reasons for the policy: The camera flash is a safety hazard for the performers and a bother to the other guests. He insisted that they had been treated rudely and that the incident had ruined their vacation. Then he demanded compensation; he said he would accept nothing less than a free vacation at the resort, plus airfare from New York.

I knew this was never going to happen. Nevertheless, I told the opportunistic young man that I would call him in a few days after I'd had a chance to look into the issue. By the time I did, he had cooled off. I said I was unable to give him exactly what he wanted and asked him to think about what else would make him happy. In the end, we agreed that the next time he planned a trip to Disney World, he would call my office so I could arrange something special for him and his girlfriend. You'll notice that at no point during this conversation did I utter the word *no*.

As a manager, you can use this strategy not only with customers, but with employee requests. Let's say you've posted the schedule for the week and then someone asks for Saturday off. You could make things easy for yourself by just saying "no." But long-term, that "no" might prove costly if the employee starts doing a shoddy job because he's upset by your attitude, or looks for a job at a company whose management is more flexible, or treats your customers the way you treated him. Instead, you could say, "Give me a day to work on this.

I'll try to get someone to take your shift." The key word is "try." If you really do try and still have to turn down the request, the employee will appreciate your effort and feel that you treated him with respect.

As I was reviewing the final draft of this book, I experienced an excellent example of never-say-no service. At the time, Priscilla and I happened to be traveling and were staying at the Kybele, a sixteen-room hotel in Istanbul. In the lounge one evening, Priscilla asked our server, a man named Yasar Cetinkaya, if they had any cookies. There were no cookies in sight and no mention of them on the menu. Instead of saying "no," Yasar asked, "With sugar, or no sugar?" Priscilla said, "With sugar." Yasar smiled and left. A few minutes later he returned, a bit out of breath, with a plate of chocolate cookies. Priscilla had a hunch that he had left the premises to get those cookies, so she asked him. Yasar confessed that he had run down the street to another hotel. End result: Priscilla got some delicious chocolate cookies, Yasar received a big tip, I got a great story, and the Kybele Hotel got a nice recommendation in this book.

The bottom line is this: It's almost always better to try to come up with a solution than to say "no" right off the bat. In my book, "no" is one of the more unpleasant words in the English language. "No problem," on the other hand, is music to my ears, just as it is to the ears of your customers.

Rule #35

Be Flexible

I often wince when I hear the term *zero tolerance*. It is frequently used to rationalize actions like expelling a child for bringing a plastic dinner knife to school or arresting a homeless person who shoplifted food. In my opinion, this policy should really be called "zero flexibility," and a lack of flexibility can be as harmful in customer service as it is in education or law. Flexibility means being open-minded. It means welcoming new ideas and alternative viewpoints. It means adapting to changed circumstances. It means bending a little to make your customer happy.

Admit it, you're not perfect. No one is. Mistakes will happen. Times will change. New information will arise. If you're not flexible enough to revise your policies and procedures, you will lose out to a competitor who is. The best managers are not only open-minded, they are gluttons for new ideas. They are not only adaptable, they are actually eager to improve the way things are done—quickly, if not immediately. Someone once defined a great leader as a person "of fixed and unbending principles, the first of which is to be flexible at all times."

How do you feel when you see a sign that reads "Absolutely No Returns"? When I see it, I take my business elsewhere. The sign tells me the company is inflexible and unwilling to take the time and energy to listen to my complaints. They may think they have good reason to adopt that policy. Maybe their product is the kind that customers can easily use and then return, essentially getting a free rental. Maybe they've been taken advantage of in the past. To me, it doesn't matter. There are other ways to address those concerns than to alienate customers with an inflexible policy.

Today's consumer enjoys a dizzying and ever-changing array of options for just about every need you can think of. Smart businesses know that their procedures have to be as elastic as the marketplace. This is why insurance companies advertise flex benefits. It's why companies offer flex work schedules. It's why retailers promote flexible payment plans. Remember Burger King's "Have It Your Way" campaign? There's a good reason their business fell off once they abandoned that slogan. The customers' response was clear: Do it my way and I'll come back; make me do it your way, and the only back you'll see is mine as I walk out the door. After their course correction, Burger King expanded all around the world. Not long ago, I walked by one of their outlets in Istanbul, and it was packed. They are obviously doing it the way the Turks want it done.

Of course, it's often easier to adopt a "zero flexibility" policy with your customers. If you're rigid, you don't have to listen to them so much; you don't have to think about what they tell you; you don't have to make decisions about specific issues or think up creative ways to handle unusual problems. But it is not the way to build trust and loyalty. You can accomplish that only by being flexible enough to treat each customer—and situation—as an individual, and an important one at that.

To a certain degree, flexibility is a personality trait. Some people are programmed, either by genetics or by upbringing, to be more conservative, cautious, and slow to change; others are more inherently open, adaptable, and eager to try new things. Each set of traits has its virtues, but if you take either tendency too far, you run into trouble. It's true that in some cases, sticking to tradition and standard operating procedures can be wise, and approaching change with caution can be prudent. But if you're always rigid and unyielding, the train will pass you by. Customers simply don't like dealing with stubborn, uncompromising people who won't bend an inch. Take it from the most successful coach in college basketball history, the legendary John Wooden: "An effective leader allows exceptions to the rule for exceptional results or when circumstance demands."

More than one company has lost my business with inflexible policies. I once exchanged a printer at an office supply company, only to find that it used different ink cartridges from the ones I'd bought for the previous model. I called and asked if I could return my unused cartridges. I was told I could, but when I got to the store they said I could have only a store credit or a gift card. No cash. No credit card refund. Why? Because that's their policy. And why is it their policy? The person at the desk had no idea, and that's exactly my point. The shortsighted folks at corporate headquarters hadn't given her the flexibility to stray from their rigid policy—even when it meant potentially losing a customer. They didn't even give her the information to explain why she couldn't.

An ancient Chinese proverb advises leaders to be like bamboo: strong, sturdy, and firmly rooted, but capable of bending with the breeze. Whether you're a leader or not, providing outstanding service should be your unyielding mission; how you fulfill that mission should be as flexible as bamboo.

Rule #36

Apologize Like You Really Mean It

"I'm sorry." Have you ever noticed how everything changes when someone utters that simple phrase? As with "please" and "thank you," its impact is almost magical. So please, make sure it's part of your service vocabulary.

When you make a mistake, telling a customer "I'm sorry" is necessary, but by itself it is not enough. *How* you say those magic words matters just as much. Sincere apologies can't be produced by formula, and they can't be programmed into a computer. Apologizing as though you really mean it is more of an art form than a science. That said, here are some general tips for making a genuine apology:

* Acknowledge exactly what happened. Do not issue a generic apology. It's important that the offended parties know you understand *why* they

are upset. So do your homework and make sure you're apologizing for the right thing. Find out the relevant details and address the specific events that upset the customer.

★ Take responsibility. Examine objectively how you personally contributed to the mishap, or what the people who report to you did, then own up to it.

★ Time it wisely. Some apologies should be made as quickly as possible, while others ought to be delayed. It is wise to wait, for instance, if you need time to do some detective work about what went wrong. Sometimes, depending on his or her level of anger, it can be a good idea to give an unhappy customer an hour or two—or a day or two—to simmer down and be able to hear what you have to say.

★ Choose the right medium for your message. Where and how you apologize also matters. In some instances—a long-standing relationship with a valued client, for example—the apology should be made in person, perhaps over lunch or dinner (on you, of course). For a less personal relationship, a phone call, a letter, a handwritten note, an e-mail, or even a text message might suffice. The main factors to consider when choosing the medium for your apology should be the strength and history of the relationship and of course the severity of the damage.

* Make it brief and unambiguous. No excuses. No elaborate explanations. Get right to the point.
* Reassure them it will not happen again. You might not be able to guarantee a mistake-free future, but you *can* guarantee that you will take action to prevent a recurrence of what went wrong in a specific instance.
* Offer restitution. Try to come up with something of value—a credit, a gift certificate, free shipping, an upgrade, and so on—to help make amends.
* Be sincere. Nothing matters more than this. People can tell when you're spouting empty words or saying you're sorry just because it's expected of you. Make sure the customer knows you truly mean it. What if you don't? What if you think the situation doesn't really warrant an apology or that the mistake was the customer's, not yours? Then it's time to trot out those acting skills, because if the customer needs a sincere apology, it's your job to convince him or her that you're truly sorry. A comedian once said, "The most important thing is sincerity. If you can fake that, you've got it made." Well, you don't want to go that far, but if you try putting yourself in the shoes of the customer and recognize that he or she has reason to be upset, it will be a lot easier to deliver a sincere and humble apology.

Remember the Elton John song "Sorry Seems to Be the Hardest Word"? If you feel that way, my advice is, *get over it*. Everything is hard before it is easy. A sincere "I'm sorry" is a small investment, and the returns can be huge.

Rule #37

Surprise Them with Something Extra

The checkout people at our local Publix supermarket always ask, "Did you find everything you were looking for?" Ninety-nine percent of the time, our answer is, "Yes." One day, Priscilla said, "No, you don't have the graham cracker mix I normally use. I'm making a key lime pie." She settled for her second choice and went home. Less than an hour later, our doorbell rang. To my utter surprise, it was a Publix employee holding a box of Priscilla's preferred brand. I don't know if he found it in a storeroom, or at another supermarket, or someplace else, but what matters is, he went the extra mile to make us happy—and then some.

A former colleague of mine told me a similar story. She had picked up a takeout sandwich from Chick-fil-A. When she got home, she found that the french fries were not in the bag. Disappointed, she called the store. The manager apologized for the oversight and asked for her address. "I assumed it was so he could send me a coupon for free fries," she told me. "But a half hour later a Chick-fil-A employee came to my door with a *huge* bag of fries! I was stunned!" She added, "That one encounter has made me a loyal customer ever since." She now tells that story to new employees at her own company as an example of how to surprise and delight a customer. No matter what you think of Chick-fil-A's politics, that's good service.

We all love the surprise of getting something extra when it's not expected. I'm sure you remember being excited about finding an extra prize in a box of Cracker Jack or the thrill of getting a brightly wrapped present when it wasn't a special day. What about the nice woman at the farmers' market who throws in an extra plum? The gas station attendant who cleans your windshield when you're at the self-service pump? The bakery that lets you sample a cookie? They're not just being generous; they know that the cost of those little surprises is nothing compared with the revenue they get from repeat customers. The practice is probably as old as commerce itself. You know the term *baker's dozen*? It was coined hundreds of years ago, when bakers in England added a thirteenth loaf of bread to a purchase of twelve.

This isn't rocket science. Actually, it's brain science. In 2011, neuroscientists confirmed the wisdom of the ages when they found evidence that our brains crave the excitement of surprise. It seems that the region of the brain called the nucleus accumbens, aka the pleasure center, experiences more activation when a pleasurable stimulus comes unexpectedly than it does when the same pleasure is predictable. As the lead researcher on the brain-imaging study, Dr. Gregory Berns of Emory University, explained it, "So if you get a present for your birthday, that's nice. But you'll like it a lot more if you get a present and it's not your birthday." That's why the same beer tastes better when a bartender gives you a free one out of the blue than it does when the bar advertises "two for one."

There are countless ways to give a little extra service, and many of them will cost you little or nothing. You can take more time with a customer. You can offer her a cup of coffee. You can make a contribution to his favorite charity. Once, the general manager of a hotel I often stayed at surprised me with a bottle of my favorite wine. How did he know it was my favorite? He called my home and consulted with Priscilla.

During the months of writing this book, I asked virtually everyone I came into contact with to e-mail me stories about a time they received stupendous service. Almost every story I received involved a company surprising the customer with something extra. Some were simple gestures, like the RadioShack employee who, after fetching the battery a customer needed for a certain gadget, offered to put the battery in the device. Others were more elaborate, such as the owner of an independent bookstore who, upon realizing she didn't have a particular book that a customer wanted to give his child for Christmas, phoned her chief competitor and had them set aside a copy for the man. Then there was the service rep who stayed on the phone longer than she needed to because the customer who'd called was housebound owing to a severe medical condition and was obviously lonely. The next day, the customer was stunned to receive "an enormous bouquet of lilies and roses" from the company, along with a personal note wishing her a speedy recovery and an upgrade that entitled her to free delivery on subsequent orders.

That company was Zappos. I've heard a lot of great above-and-beyond stories about that online retailer, which has what *Businessweek* magazine called "a near-fanatical devotion to customer service." For example, there was the time a guy ordered a specific pair of shoes he had to wear as best man at a wedding. UPS messed up the shipment, and the shoes didn't arrive before he left for the airport to fly to the wedding site. What did Zappos do? They sent a replacement pair overnight to the customer's destination. Not only did they cover the charge for shipping, they gave him a complete refund.

With a bit of imagination, you too can delight customers by giving them a little extra when they least expect it. They'll surprise you in return by coming back early and often and by singing your praises to others.

Keep Doing It Better

S atchel Paige, the legendary baseball pitcher, once said, "Don't look back. Something might be gaining on you." That's good business advice. If you get too satisfied with your past achievements, your competitors will gain on you fast. Your customers might love you today, but as the song goes, will they still love you tomorrow? Not if another company finds ways to serve them better while you rest on your laurels.

Great companies have the mentality of champion athletes and great artists and visionary inventors: they never stop searching for ways to improve. If you want your business to be known for customer service, every employee should constantly be looking for ways to do it better tomorrow than they do it today—and to keep on doing it even better next week, next month, next year. Every one of the Customer Rules is about doing it better, and every one is a never-ending process, not a one-off. If you believe you have already reached the pinnacle, it is only a matter of time before you'll be asking, "Where have all the customers gone?"

Better is not a destination; it is a journey. You never arrive at better; it is always in the future, because there is always an even better way to serve your customers. So strive to be moving constantly in that direction, and never look back. Although you might be doing it as well as it can possibly be done today, you may find that tomorrow brings a new idea, a new procedure, a new employee, a new insight—something that raises the bar a wee bit higher. Put what you did today, yesterday, and the day before in the past, and leave it there. This is today—the day you can call your team or your staff together and have a meeting devoted entirely to one question: "How can we do it better tomorrow?"

Rule #39

Don't Try Too Hard

D id you just read the title of this chapter and think, Wait a minute. Don't try too hard? Hasn't this whole book been about trying harder to serve your customers? Well, it has, and you should. But the key word here is "too." Trying hard is important, but trying *too* hard can be as bad as not trying enough. It's kind of like parenting, where doing too much for your kids is sometimes worse than doing too little.

Think about how you feel when an overbearing salesperson in a store hovers over you and asks repeatedly if you need assistance, when all you want is to be left alone to look around. Or think how annoying it is when a server at a restaurant stops by your table every five minutes to ask if everything's okay with your meal. That behavior is so pervasive that I recently saw a cartoon that pictured a couple at home, with the wife holding the phone and telling her husband, "It's the waiter at the restaurant where we ate tonight. He wants to know if everything is still all right." Here's a tip: If your customers have to stifle the urge to scream, "Go away!" or, "Leave us alone!" you're trying too hard.

Unfortunately, the brave new world of social media has given companies additional ways to turn off customers by trying way too hard. I don't know about you, but I find it irritating when I get e-mails from companies I do business with asking me to "like" them on Facebook. Nor do I like it when companies flood my in-box with six messages a day alerting me to company news, new product arrivals, or even special offers. The occasional e-mail letting customers know about a major change in corporate policy, the opening of a new store location, or a blowout sale is fine, but any company that feels the need to contact you daily is simply trying too hard.

Nine times out of ten, trying too hard will backfire. Being overly solicitous and eager to please is not only annoying, it makes you seem phony. Customers will feel that they're being manipulated, and their guard will go up. Your intentions might be pure, but the fact is, no one likes a phony, and most people can spot one in the first few sentences you speak—sometimes even before you open your mouth. No one likes to be pestered constantly, either, and you'll lose customers quickly if you hover over them when they are clearly trying to shop in peace or enjoy a quiet dinner with a companion.

Mind you, it is not always easy for employees to know when someone wants less attention rather than more, because most customers are nice; they grin and bear it when service gets too intrusive. My rule of thumb when I worked in the restaurant business was: Don't interrupt customers who are in the middle of an intimate or intense conversation, and don't ask if they're enjoying their food before they have taken at least two or three bites. In a retail store, you might want to let the customers themselves decide how much attention they want by simply having a salesperson say, "Just let me know if I can assist you," when they enter the store.

This doesn't mean you don't have to pay attention. While customers seldom complain if you try too hard, they *do* complain if you ignore them. So train your employees to keep a keen eye on customers so they can act promptly when they want help. It's not hard to spot the signs: they stop eating and talking to their companions and lift their gaze; they step back from the merchandise and look around. I call it "the long neck, help me" look. When customers want your attention, their necks extend and rotate like a periscope. The rule is: Heads down means they don't need you; heads up means just that—they are giving you a heads-up to come and serve them.

Bottom line is, if your service is truly superior, you won't *have* to try so hard. Take it from me: If you follow the thirty-nine Customer Rules in this book and do your part to make sure everyone in your organization follows them, giving your customers authentically great service will be as easy and effortless as giving your children love.

ACKNOWLEDGMENTS

I thank:

My family first and foremost . . . Priscilla, Daniel, Valerie, Jullian, Margot, and Tristan.

Phil Goldberg for bringing my Customer Rules to the light of day.

Talia Krohn for being our super editor at Random House. You are the best.

Roger Scholl at Random House for encouraging me to write this book.

Lynn Franklin for being a terrific literary agent and special friend.

All of my teachers at Hilton, Marriott, and Disney who taught me the Customer Rules.

All of those around the world who really understand service and are the giving ones—especially our military.

Special note to my three grandchildren, Margot, Jullian, and Tristan: *Don't forget our family rules and the things you promised to do!*

If you want to learn more . . .

The principles, strategies, and techniques that Lee discusses in his two books, *The Customer Rules* and *Creating Magic*, are incorporated into the speeches and seminars he gives around the world. Presentations are always customized to the specific organization involved, but here are some examples of his most popular talks.

The Customer Rules

Learn how to apply the 39 Essential Rules for Delivering Sensational Service to your customers, clients, patients, passengers, and guests.

You Can Create Magic *Too*!

Great leaders understand what their fellow team members want the most and how to provide it to them. They are rewarded with a healthy organization, excellent results, and—yes—a magical experience for their customers.

Creating Magic: 10 Common Sense Leadership Strategies from a Life at Disney

Learn how to apply the strategies to your business. At Disney, it is not the magic that makes it work; it's the way we work that makes it magic. Based on Lee's first book, *Creating Magic*. Available everywhere books are sold.

It's Your Life: Time/Life Management

Learn how to put more control into all parts of your life through this simple system for planning and carrying out your responsibilities. Lee has taught this seminar for over thirty years to more than one hundred thousand attendees, with extraordinary success.

A Day of Learning

Give Lee a day to present three powerful seminars to your organization's leaders and dramatically improve their abilities as managers, parents, citizens, and leaders.

**Creating Magic: 10 Common Sense
Leadership Strategies from a Life at Disney**

The Customer Rules

It's Your Life: Time/Life Management

*These seminars are based on the principles taught at
the world-renowned Disney Institute.*

For more information and complete contact information, please
visit Lee's website: www.LeeCockerell.com.

INDEX

computer repair, 125–26, 127, 133–34
computer simulation, 55
copycatting, 86–91
copying ideas, 86–91
Covey, Stephen, 84–85
Creating Magic (Cockerell), xi, 102, 182, 183
customer service
  apologies, 168–71
  availability, 99–100
  basic truth of, ix–xi
  defined, 3
  emotional aspect, 124
  Golden Rule, 65
  handling complaints, 77–78
  as personal responsibility, 1–4
  practicing selflessness, 108–10, 174–75
  resolving problems, 148–51
  role of commitment, 41
  top-down approach, 9–12
  triple crown, 41
  trying too hard, 178–80
customers
  angry, 156–58
  anticipating needs, 111–13
  "bad," no such thing, 154–55
  being ignored, 123–25
  keeping promises to, 114–18
  leaving lasting impression, 63–65
  making feel special, 121–22
  needs *vs.* wants, 129–34
  never arguing with, 161–63

  treating as VIPs, 61–67
  words for speaking of, 96–98

Dare, Bud, 25
Davis, Bud, 152–53, 154
Denning, Stephen, xiii
Disney, Walt, 15, 69
Disney World, 4, 10, 25–26, 42–43, 51, 55, 59–60, 69–70, 71, 102, 150, 161
Disneyland, 10, 69

Eastern Air Lines, 96
ecosystems, 24–27
Edison, Thomas, 34
Einstein, Albert, 74
employees
  availability for customer service, 99–104
  brainstorming new products and services, 113
  colleagues as friendly competitors, 60
  hiring, 37–41
  interviewing prospects, 37–41
  mastering basics, 13–18
  scripts for, 42–46
  words for speaking of, 95–96
energy, 30–31
expectations, high, 57–60
expertise, 71–72

Facebook, 179
FedEx, 139